CISG and the Unification of International Trade Law

Critically examining the assumption that the creation of a convention introduces a uniform law and that conventions contribute to harmonisation of international laws, this work examines the Convention for the International Sale of Goods (CISG) by investigating how far international jurisprudence has advanced and whether such a development can truly be considered a harmonisation or unification. Zeller 'pushes the boundaries' of unification of international sales laws at the expense of domestic laws, with the aim of fostering debate as to how far the boundaries of unification can be pushed.

The gap-filling role of domestic courts is also considered. By gauging the importance of domestic involvement in cases, which essentially fall under the auspices of the CISG, Zeller considers whether unification is merely a myth and his findings prove invaluable to future development of unified laws.

Dr Bruno Zeller, B.Com (Melbourne), B.Ed (Melbourne), Master of International Trade Law (Deakin), PhD in Law (Melbourne), Arbitrator (AICA), is Senior Lecturer at Victoria University, Melbourne, and Adjunct Professor at Murdoch University, Perth.

CISG and the Unification of International Trade Law

Bruno Zeller

Routledge
Taylor & Francis Group
LONDON AND NEW YORK

First published 2007 by
Routledge-Cavendish

Published 2014 by
Routledge
2 Park Square, Milton Park, Abingdon, Oxon OX14 4RN

Simultaneously published in the USA and Canada
by Routledge
711 Third Ave, New York, NY 10017

Routledge is an imprint of the Taylor & Francis Group, an informa business

Typeset in Times New Roman by
Newgen Imaging Systems (P) Ltd, Chennai, India

British Library Cataloguing in Publication Data
A catalogue record for this book is available from the British Library

Library of Congress Cataloging in Publication Data
A catalog record for this book has been requested

ISBN10: 1–84568–046–4 (hbk)
ISBN10: 0–415–42173–X (pbk)

ISBN13: 978–1–84568–046–6 (hbk)
ISBN13: 978–0–415–42173–7 (pbk)

Contents

Acknowledgements

Not a single book would ever be written without the help of colleagues. I would like to thank Al Kritzer of Pace University School of Law, New York who read an earlier draft and made some useful suggestions.

However most importantly my thanks must go to Christiana Fountoulakis of Basel University School of Law who not only read the entire book but also made some valuable contribution by adding and subtracting ideas and also by suggesting useful references. It must be noted that Christiana did not agree with all the ideas and expressed some reservations but her help has been greatly appreciated. Without her help the book would not be in its present form. I would also like to thank Christiana's research assistant Sonja Voegelin who worked on the footnotes and bibliography and was of enormous help. Any errors are my own and all controversies are of course also to be attributed to me.

I would also like to acknowledge the help given to me by my wife Pam who puts up with the necessary single-minded pursuit of writing.

Table of cases and documents

Cases

Australia

Air Link Pty Limited v Paterson [2005] HCA 39 (10 August 2005) 37
Kotsambasis v Singapore Airlines Ltd Matter No CA 40154/96 (13 August 1997) [http://www.austlii.edu.au] 102
Laminex (Aust) Pty Ltd v Coe Manufacturing Co [1999] NSWCA 370 44
Mendelsohn-Zeller Inc v T & C Providores Ltd [1981] 1 NSWLR 366 44
Olex Focas Pty Ltd v Skodaexport Co Ltd [1998] 3 VR 380 44
Povey v Qantas Airways Ltd (2005) 79 ALJR 1215 100
Roder Zelt- und Hallenkonstruktionen GmbH v Rosedown Park Pty Ltd et al [1993] [http://cisgw3.law.pace.edu/cases/950428a2.html] 104
The Shipping Corporation of India Ltd v Gamlen Chemical Co [1980] 147 CLR 142 102

Austria

Austrian Supreme Court, Oberster Gerichtshof, 14 January 2002, 7 Ob 301/01t [http://cisgw3.law.pace.edu/cases/020114a.3.html] 61
Vienna Arbitration Proceeding, SCH-4318, 15 June 1994 [http://cisg3.law.pace.edu/cases/940615a4.html] 35

Canada

La San Guiseppe v Forti Moulding Canada 31 August 1999 Ontario Superior Court of Justice [http://cisgw3.law.pace.edu/cases/990831c4.html] 103
Nova Tool & Mold Inc v London Industries Inc [1998] O.J. No. 5381, 84 A.C.W.S. (3rd) 1089 103
Tolofson v Jensen Canadian Supreme Court [1994] 3 S.C.R 1022 27

Germany

Appellate Court of Hamm, Germany, 9 June 1995, 11 U 191/94191/94 [http://cisgw3.law.pace.edu/cases/950609g1.html] 61

ICC

Italy

Mexico

Netherlands

Russia

Switzerland

UK

USA

Documents

Chapter 1

Introduction

This book starts with the premise that unification of law serves a useful purpose. This is so because internationalisation or globalisation has in effect forced the law to take a more global approach. As trade increasingly crosses borders so by necessity has the law. Transplantations, the drafting of model laws and ratification of conventions are the responses of legal systems to internationalisation and are occurring at an increased pace.

In an ideal world one law would be applicable to cover all transactions of a similar nature wherever they occur. This unfortunately is not the case, nor will it eventuate in the foreseeable future. Municipal interests and 'sacred cows' will always be stumbling blocks to the unification process. However international conventions in discrete areas of law are the 'next best thing' in the process of creating a global law. However even international conventions are not codes and hence do not cover a complete area of law. Domestic law is always needed to fill the resulting gaps. The unification process is curtailed as soon as domestic law needs to be applied. This book takes a hard look at the confluence of the spheres of influence of a convention and domestic laws.

For the purpose of showing that unification is desirable, the Convention on Contracts for the International Sale of Goods (CISG) will be analysed. One of the reasons is that, unlike earlier conventions, the CISG included a definitional section in its regime, namely article 7. This article is the most significant development as it not only assists to define the instrument itself but it also sets the borderline of influence between the CISG and the application of domestic law. This is so because – as pointed out above – the CISG is not a code and hence gaps exist, which by definition need to be filled by municipal laws.

Many authors and tribunals have examined the extent to which the CISG is applicable and which areas are excluded from its scope. The internal boundaries of the CISG have arguably been well defined. In other words, what is and what is not governed by the CISG can be easily discovered by examining jurisprudence and academic writing.

What this book attempts to achieve is to boldly 'push the boundaries' of unification of international sales laws at the expense of domestic laws. It is not suggested nor is it the intention of the author to find universal agreement. As the title of the book suggests, the idea is to be controversial. No doubt some of the suggestions in this book will be dismissed as either going too far, or being untenable, or even lacking credibility. If that is so and rebuttals are written, one of the aims of this book would have been achieved, namely to foster debate as to how far the boundaries of unification can be pushed.

However it was thought to be important to at least highlight areas where a possible 'creeping unification' can take place. After all the CISG is not a dead instrument but a living one, constantly adapting to new ideas and new challenges posed by globalisation.

Some ideas are simply a push into the unknown and hopefully others will either push further or authoritatively close the gap. Professor Fountoulakis of Basel University, who has patiently read the draft, has already made some suggestions where areas of this book contradict previous writings and in her view some ideas are indeed controversial and need to be abandoned or refined. It is hoped that it is the refining process that will prevail.

The most important idea is that the dividing line between domestic and international laws cannot be fixed. It must be constantly under attack in order to find a common solution to common problems. It is indeed hoped that this book will be looked at as being thought provoking and will provide a springboard for further debate in the process of defining the legal commitments of buyers and sellers of goods towards each other.

Chapter 2

Uniformity of laws

Mapping the territory

A. Uniformity of laws

I. The twentieth century – the century of internationalisation

The internationalisation of trade has raised the question of how such trade can be conducted in the most efficient manner. There is no debate that the beginning of the twentieth century has seen some significant law reforms in the area of international trade law. The attacks on the domestically dominated system of contract law, which did not distinguish between municipal contracts and international contracts, have been fought and won by the internationalists. It is now clear that:

> ...the nineteenth century rules the liberals have been attacking form a complex intellectual system whose vitality even in the last quarter of the twentieth century is as much or more the product of its ideological power as of the direct material dominance of particular economic or political interests.[1]

As a result of the ideological shift in thinking, it has been questioned: 'why is there international uniform commercial law rather than nothing?'[2] The answer depends on who is asking the question. From a legal-philosophical point of view, the response could well be that it is a vision that could be called normative, an emphasis on a principle of thought that considers uniform laws to be a virtue.[3]

Practically speaking, it is universally accepted that legal risks and costs are reduced if there would be one law and one judiciary dealing with international trade. There is equally no debate that the creation of a single judiciary worldwide will never eventuate. Hence, the only practical possibility is the creation of a universal trade law which is applied in all or at least in most domestic courts.

1 Kennedy (1976: 1722).
2 Marquis (2005: 2).
3 Marquis (2005: 238).

One possible solution is the creation of conventions, which are open for accession by individual nations and which become part of domestic law.

This book attempts to have a fresh and contentious look at uniform laws – within the meaning of 'unified laws' – and specifically at the United Nations Convention on Contracts for the International Sale of Goods (CISG). The starting point in this investigation is the conclusion Marquis reached in his study of international uniform commercial law. He noted:

> For some time, the contemporary world has been undergoing transition. In its simplest expression, this transition expresses a changeover from modernity to a second modernity. This changeover is currently taking place. It is real and current. It represents an interval between a starting point and a target point. Moreover, the intermediate period that we are currently undergoing is marked by a strong ambivalence.[4]

Arguably, uniform laws – and the CISG is no exception – are merely progressing towards a target point but have not reached that point yet. This book will show that the CISG is still capable of being shaped and enlarged, as it is not a document frozen in time. Uniform laws are living documents, and their implementation is merely an intermediate period.

II. Uniform legislation – just the first level towards unification of laws

I. Legislation and interpretation – first and second level

The obvious key criterion to the success of such a law is that it should be uniformly applied. The drafters of the CISG attempted to facilitate uniformity by including article 7, the interpretative article, into the regime of the convention. Article 7(1) in the relevant parts states that 'regard is to be had to its international character and to the need to promote uniformity in its application and the observance of good faith'. The importance of this article is highlighted by the fact that it has been copied into various other documents.[5] The process of interpretation is pivotal in the attempt to achieve uniformity.

Despite a seemingly clear mandate and the inclusion of concise interpretative articles, uniformity of application is not guaranteed or automatically obtainable.

> Every text, however clear on its face, requires to be scrutinized in its context and in the light of the object and purpose which it is designed to serve. The conclusion which may be reached after such a scrutiny is, in most instances,

4 Marquis (2005: 233).

5 Art. 1.6 (1) UNIDROIT Principles; Art. 1:106 (1) Principles of European Contract Law.

> that the clear meaning which originally presented itself is the correct one, but this should not be used to disguise the fact that what is involved is a process of interpretation.[6]

The question which ultimately needs to be asked is whether the CISG facilitates international trade. In that sense, article 7 is 'a text system that forms a subsystem of the CISG'.[7] Even after recognising this fact, predictability and hence confidence in the CISG can only be achieved through international decisions that show at least an adequate level of uniformity.

This book also attempts to investigate how far uniformity is achievable. This – in some cases confronting – process ultimately will turn on the interpretative question of any uniform legal instrument.

2. Desirability of uniform laws

Wishing to create a new international economic order is a proposition that is either boringly old hat or is extremely original. It begs the question whether these international treaties do serve a useful purpose, namely to provide a satisfactory basis not only for international trade but also for domestic legislation.[8] To put it differently:

> If the search for uniform solutions is a good thing, then ultimately, 'Why (Not) Seek Uniform Solutions?' is a matter of understanding what should and should not be harmonized.[9]

This question is a complex one and depends on the will of the legal profession and sovereign states to abandon domestic laws in favour of a supranational one. A good example of an inward looking legal system is the United Kingdom, which was heavily involved in the design of the CISG. However, it never ratified the convention despite being a member of the EU. Although Lord Steyn in his maiden speech drew the government's attention to the fact that the United Kingdom played a 'full and constructive role' in formulating the CISG and although the Law Commission recommended ratifying the CISG, no official announcement was made. The Government's response simply was that 'it continued to take an active part in the business of the convention'.[10]

It appears that the United Kingdom is still under the impression that 'the law which applies to international commodities contracts conducted on standard form terms promulgated by London based trading associations [and therefore] the law

6 Sinclair (1984: 72–73).
7 Charters (2005: 8).
8 Hobhouse (1990: 531).
9 Walker (2002: 341).
10 Hansard, H.L. 3 May 1995, Vol. 563 cols 1457 ff.

of international sale of goods…is but English domestic law writ large'.[11] This may be true in the case of the commodities market, which has a rich history, which is dominated by very few players and which arguably developed a private language that is incomprehensible to trade outsiders.[12] It could be argued that at least in the commodities market a uniform law is applicable, namely United Kingdom law. It follows that it is of no real consequence what law is applicable to the rest of the business community that is not involved in the closed trade of commodities. All involved parties within the trade understand the law and, hence, predictability and certainty is the product of a uniform law, which is applied in this case.

This is not to say that the CISG could not perform the same function, but at this stage, the convention is expressly excluded in standard commodity contracts. The problem with the above argument is that it is extremely ethnocentric and does not take into account that a globalised world may demand a different approach.

As far as the trade in manufactured goods is concerned, English law is far from being the dominant force it once was. What makes the matter worse for English traders is that they are frequently involved in litigation or arbitration where the CISG is governing law. The uniform international sales law is being interpreted and applied by courts other than English ones, and hence, the prospect of an influential interpretation of the CISG by English courts is diminished, as the United Kingdom has not ratified the CISG.[13] Bridge argues that:

> To cast all of that experience [in commodities contracts] aside in place of something that is incomplete and untested would be wasteful and destructive. The practical concerns of English law in the area of commodity contracts are a world away from those arising out of the type of contract facing a court or arbitrator applying the CISG.[14]

To argue that a commodities contract is specialised and a 'world away' from other economic activities and for that reason should not be subject to a uniform law is not helpful. Schwenzer correctly argued that the problem with an approach as advocated by Bridge amounts to a 'breach categorization'.[15] Simply put, the CISG does provide a means by solving any dispute, including commodity sale, 'in a reasonable manner that extends beyond the narrow confines of national pre-conceived views'.[16]

If every country would adopt the same attitude, the introduction of a unified law would be impossible. Most trading nations have understood that it is more

11 Bridge (1997: 277).
12 See Leible (1998: 289).
13 Bridge (1997: 278).
14 Bridge (1997: 279).
15 Schwenzer (2005: 800).
16 Schwenzer (2005: 800).

helpful to their trade and economy to adopt and ratify a convention than to insist that their well-tested domestic law is superior to an untested convention.

It is also worth noting that commodities contracts are known to be strict and interpreted literally. As Bridge noted, commodities sales involve a 'hair trigger right of termination'.[17] Such endeavours are normally defended as being necessary to promote certainty. A case may illustrate this point, namely *The New Prosper*.[18] The case involved the sale of Australian barley. Under the contract, the buyer had to nominate a ship and the seller had the right to nominate a port from an agreed range. The buyer nominated the *New Prosper*, which was rejected by the seller on the grounds that it could not load the ship due to local restrictions in one of the ports allowed under the contract. The literal interpretation of the contractual clause allowed the seller to cancel the contract. The apparent reason the seller rejected the boat was simply to avoid the contract and take advantage of a rise in the market price. It was not the inability to ship the goods, which could have been loaded without any problems from another conforming port. It would be interesting to speculate whether the CISG would have come to the same conclusion by invoking articles 8 and 9.

There is no debate that in the commodities market, strict standards do apply, especially where the problem of timely delivery is concerned. Therefore, the handing over of clean documents is always of the essence to the contract, and to cure any defects in the documentation does not extend to commodities markets.[19] The solution under the CISG would be comparable to any domestic law, as in this instance, the perfect tender rule as known in common law can also be applied under the CISG by taking customary practices[20] and the intent of the parties[21] into consideration.

The CISG, in conjunction with the International Commercial Terms (INCOTERMS) and the Uniform Customs and Practices (UCP 500), offers a viable solution to commodity traders. It plays a supplementary role, and preconceived domestic views to the contrary must be rejected.[22]

B. Explicit exclusion of the CISG – a step in the wrong direction?

I. The critics' voice

A further point needs to be discussed at the beginning. There have been suggestions that the CISG does not contribute towards uniformity and is not an

17 Bridge (2003: 68).
18 *Richco International Ltd v Bunge & Co Ltd* [1991] 2 Lloyd's Rep. 93.
19 Schwenzer (2005: 806).
20 Art. 9.
21 Art. 8.
22 Schwenzer (2005: 807).

important regime in practice.[23] One of the reasons is that the CISG is often excluded in general conditions, such as by large Dutch companies, as 'there is apparently no need to make use of it as national legal systems already fulfil these parties' needs'.[24] The fact simply is that such a statement is backward looking. It ignores the trend to support uniform laws, which have the capacity to solve international disputes. It further ignores the fact that a new generation of lawyers is being educated and at one stage a critical mass of internationally informed legal practitioners will take a completely different view on what will 'fulfill the parties' needs' in international trade.

II. The character of the CISG

1. Building bridges

Conventions are a world apart from domestic laws, and the differences must be understood to fully appreciate the value of an international unified law. The first observation is that conventions are not codes; they are, by necessity, political instruments, a compromise of the desires of the various and diverse drafters, though the 'texts themselves often represent masterpieces of diplomatic negotiations and draftsmanship'.[25]

The compromises in the drafting stage ran along many dimensions, such as between civil law and common law, between developed and developing nations and the old Soviet Bloc and North/South/East and West.[26] With the demise of the Soviet Bloc and the change in the strategic development of China, and with the increased emergence of independent states, it is obvious that the CISG is not a compromise along ideological lines but a compromise among markets and regulations.

> [The CISG is] a unified picture going forward – that steps out of the paradigms of conflict along spectrums. The Convention thus adopts a flexible structure that allows for interpretation in light of whatever type of social-political-economic system is prevalent at the time.[27]

Simply put, the CISG is not an instrument that was developed in 1988 and is now 'frozen in time'. On the contrary, article 7 specifically allows the convention to adapt to changing market situations and is, therefore, a sales law for the 'real world'.

23 Smits (2005: 161).
24 Smits (2005: 161).
25 Hobhouse (1990: 531).
26 Charters (2005: 15).
27 Charters (2005: 17).

It is, arguably, for the above reasons that the Convention has been ratified by many nations and integrated into the municipal system of laws. Two problems can be readily discovered. The first one is that domestic courts are interpreting international instruments; despite the mandate of article 7, ethnocentric interpretation is and will remain a concern.

2. *Being incomplete – a quality!*

The second problem is that since conventions are not codes, gaps within the Convention will exist. It has been argued that the reason for such phenomena is the fact that conventions are seeking to legislate for the ordinary law, such as sales law, and often 'do so in a piecemeal fashion'.[28] The question is whether gap filling significantly alters outcomes of disputes, thereby rendering uniformity of application impossible, since outcomes are determined by choice of laws.

The CISG, as pointed out above, incorporated its own mandate in relation to an interpretation of the Convention. On face value, the corner stone in a process of 'sameness' of interpretation by all those who need to apply the Convention has been laid. However, as municipal law is still relevant and needs to work side by side with the CISG, harmonisation or unification can only be superficial, especially if the need of the commercial community has not been met. After all, the law in general is merely the means or the tool to conduct commercial activities effectively and efficiently.[29]

Hobhouse noted that, since the CISG is a multicultural compromise,

> ... [the principles underpinning the CISG] will normally have less merit than most of the individual legal systems from which they have been derived. They lack coherence and consistency. They create problems about their scope. They introduce uncertainty where no uncertainty existed before. They probably deprive the law of those features which enable it to be an effective tool for the use of international commerce.[30]

This view exhibits an ethnocentric interpretation of international trade and ignores the ability of the law to change and adapt. After all, laws are merely expressions of the culture of a society. In the twenty-first century, globalisation and internationalisation appears to be the culture of commerce, and it makes sense to step away from municipal law and create an international one.

Hobhouse is correct to argue that uncertainty can emerge. However, this is only the case if no uniform interpretation of the CISG has been achieved. Furthermore, as Hobhouse himself states, the law is merely a tool, and as with

28 Hobhouse (1990: 532).
29 Hobhouse (1990: 532).
30 Hobhouse (1990: 532).

most tools, they are only as good as the hands that use them. Hobhouse wrote in 1990 and significant advances have been made since then. There is a vast jurisprudence available, let alone academic writing. However, the question of whether the CISG has brought harmonisation or unification to international trade law is still debated. It is correct to note that any new law, municipal or international, needs a 'bedding in' time in order to be understood.

Interestingly enough, Hobhouse also stated that 'the utopian ideals which have led to the present situation have a parallel in those which gave rise to the movement for the adoption of Esperanto as a universal language'.[31] It is true to say that Esperanto was hailed as the lingua franca, and it is also true to say that it has not lived up to its expectations. However, Hobhouse was wrong to suggest that international laws are utopian; reality today shows that they are anything but that. Globalisation and internationalisation of commerce is best served not by commercial competition and choice of laws but by a system that is universally applicable and not restricted by jurisdictional boundaries. International trade and globalisation do not know any borders, nor are they limited by legal jurisdictions. One example will highlight the problem. If a dispute arose in the United Kingdom – one single political structure – the question still needs to be asked whether English or Scottish laws apply. Is it not simpler for an international corporation merely to be bound by a law which is applicable in most of the world instead of having to wonder which of the municipal laws within one political structure applies?

Unfortunately, ethnocentricity was well alive in 1990 and is so till today:

> Only conventions which demonstrably satisfy the well-proven needs of the commercial community should be ratified and legislation should only be agreed to if it is demonstrably fit to be enacted as part of the municipal law of this country.[32]

If that view prevailed, no international conventions would ever have been written, let alone be adopted. It is impossible to gauge the success of a law until it has been applied. Specifically those who are closely affected by it must have had a chance of experiencing the influence of the new regime and passing judgment on it. The success of the CISG has prompted some scholars to coin the phrase that international trade is a 'bifocal world' divided into 'Vienna and Non-Vienna' legal structures.[33]

The CISG is not a complete statement of sales laws. It must be considered that most of its gaps are not the result of an oversight of the drafters or a lack of trying to comprehensively cover the subject matter but rather the result of vested interests. Compromise cannot be achieved in all areas.[34] Therefore, arguably,

31 Hobhouse (1990: 525).
32 Hobhouse (1990: 535).
33 Bridge (1997).
34 Consumer protection laws are a clear example of this particular problem.

only laws which are demonstrably fit to be enacted as part of the municipal law[35] are included into the regime of the CISG. The CISG had to accommodate 'important domestic policies that outweigh common international interests'.[36] The interplay between domestic rules which desire to protect some classes of persons and the need to streamline and standardise rules to govern international trade[37] has been played out at the Diplomatic Conference. The result of such interplay is the CISG, and it is important to find the boundaries where unified laws will inevitably collide with domestic legal systems.

It is for this reason that an investigation into the existence of gaps and their filling has been undertaken. It will highlight how successful or harmonious a convention can be or whether disharmony is created in at least some aspects of the law. Marquis succinctly argued that:

> ...contrary to appearances, expanded and fragmented uniform law appears to be eminently practical. It is capable of identifying the true issues, the actual problematic and the most likely components of a solution.[38]

The question must be asked whether the CISG achieved the tasks set by the promoters of the convention. This book, therefore, will investigate in what areas unification has not been fully achieved and attempt to suggest possible solutions.

The first task will be devoted to an understanding of harmonisation or uniformity. These terms are frequently used synonymously; however, this book will show that they are not interchangeable, that harmonisation is simply a myth and that it is unification of laws which is the important outcome the CISG attempts to achieve.

C. Harmonisation or unification

I. Distinguishing between unification and harmonisation

Whether harmonisation or unification is at issue, the fact is that the true purpose of such a discussion will inevitably turn to the question of law reform.

If we consider interjurisdictional private transactions, a diversity of laws has been found to be detrimental to the development of global trade. A uniformity of law is the desired outcome. The simple tool is to merely transplant an existing law borrowed from another system into a domestic one. Transplantation of laws is a way to speed up law reforms by avoiding the natural evolution of laws.

Of course, the question will be asked whether transplantation is synonymous with the ratification of international instruments. The answer must be: it

35 Hobhouse (1990: 535).
36 Kastely (1988: 590).
37 Hartnell (1993: 1).
38 Marquis (2005: 236).

depends. This book will use the term transplantation only in those circumstances where a legal system rewrites a law in such a way that it is the same or nearly identical to the one from which it is borrowed.

A ratification of an international instrument, on the other hand, is termed as a unification of laws, since it entails an introduction of a set of laws that are written not by parliamentary draftsmen, but by an international body of legal experts and accepted in an international conference. Furthermore, and in contrast to transplantation, this set of rules is not open to domestic change, despite the fact that it has become part of a domestic system by virtue of its ratification. Changes can only be implemented by a diplomatic conference, thus preserving uniformity.

At this point, a clear distinction must be drawn between the process of harmonisation and unification of law. Harmonisation is a process of making rules similar, whereas unification aims at the sameness of rules. Of course, there is an interaction between harmonising and unifying law. Arguably, harmonisation is the first, prudent step towards uniform solutions. Intense comparative studies are the first step in harmonising laws. This does not suggest that comparative law is not a useful tool in the creation of conventions. On the contrary, conventions are born from the work of comparative studies; otherwise, consent amongst jurists of diverse backgrounds could not be achieved. However, unification processes can often be based on the result of harmonised laws; the theoretical background research often will have already taken place, namely when analysing which parts of the law lend themselves to harmonisation. This has led Linarelli to the sceptical vote: 'harmonisation literature is a "theory-rich" environment, where it seems that if one theory does not fit, another stands ready'.[39]

However, Boodman[40] suggests that harmonisation is a construct of comparative law. As jurists with diverse origins communicate intelligibly about private interjurisdictional transactions, the notion of harmonisation adds nothing to the discourse.[41]

II. Which one to prefer?

1. The controversy

This book suggests that harmonisation is good, and unification better. It is understood that an internal harmonisation of any instrument of law is essential for being accepted and contributing towards efficient solutions of legal disputes. However, it is argued that once a law has been developed and has been

39 Linarelli (2002: 339).
40 Boodman (1991: 707).
41 Boodman (1991: 705).

considered to be acceptable, it can be used to displace a domestic law or be added to a domestic system. Once such a step has been taken, possible diversities of laws between systems have been eliminated and hence the laws in this particular field of transactions have been unified.[42]

Another perceived problem of harmonisation is that 'uniformity is not its goal, since law is conceived in terms of process rather than result and variable results are entirely compatible with the process sought to be created. . . . Laws [therefore] are not seen as conflicting; they simply co-exist as potential sources.'[43] If the world would consist of one single trade law – has the law been harmonised or has it been unified? Arguably the answer is unification. This is so because all the possible solutions within domestic systems have been unified to form one unitary system of law. Unification follows a grammatical explanation of the event that words are to be interpreted on the same level. A practical unification is to follow and a sameness of results suggests a unified system. Harmonisation may at best describe the process by which unification has been achieved. But at the end – and from a practical point of view – it is the result of unification (the unified law) that is of interest to lawyers and traders.

There is a further argument to be considered which runs contrary to unification. Jurists, notably in England and to a lesser degree in the United States, believe that it should be left to the market to decide whether the 'commercial world prefers the familiar certainties of English law or the Utopian and unpredictable ideals of Conventions'.[44] The argument is that unification of law is not important since their domestic system, namely the common law via the Commercial Court in London, is in effect the compromise solution for parties who cannot agree on a governing law. A paramount need of the commercial community, namely certainty, would be best served by one coherent system rather than through a convention, which is a 'multicultural compromise' and, therefore, lacking coherence and consistency.[45] It is an inability on their part to recognise that such views are untenable, as comparative law offers the only way by which laws can become international.[46] Consequently, such international uniformity will exhibit coherence and consistency.

2. *A look behind*

As far as unified laws are concerned, history is being repeated. Roman law was the essential source of law on the continent of Europe and disappeared only in the eighteenth century.[47] Many countries undertook 'massive transplants' in their

42 Boodman (1991: 705).
43 Glenn (1989: 783).
44 Nicholas (1993: 2).
45 Nicholas (1993: 2).
46 Zweigert and Kötz (1998: 15).
47 Zweigert and Kötz (1998: 15).

modernisation, such as the introduction of the German '*Bürgerliches Gesetzbuch*' into Japan.[48] As an interesting sideline, the only successful attempt to transplant Common Law was in the context of colonialisation.[49]

Some scholars have argued that a 'common law' is not achievable simply by a process of unification, harmonisation, or transplantation.[50] Such a view may be correct if attempts at the creation of a unified or common law are directed at a total body of law. Differences in political or social organisation need to be overcome to achieve such unification. Not surprisingly, one point of view states:

> [It] is not only useless, but dangerous to extend attempts at harmonization into fields in which legal differences reflect differences in political or social organization or in cultural or social mores.[51]

However, evidence supports the view that laws have been transplanted successfully and such a movement of a rule or a system from one state to another has been common in history.[52] Watson has argued that:

> Law develops by transplanting, not because some such rule was the inevitable consequence of the social structure and would have emerged even without a model to copy, but because the foreign rule was known to those with control over law making and they observed the [apparent] benefits which could be derived from it. What is borrowed that is to say, is very often the idea.[53]

It is exactly for these reasons that Rabel has succeeded in proposing a unified model law. Today, many successful conventions and model laws are enshrined in legislation. It is important that a distinction is made at unification of a total system and harmonisation or unification of a segment of the legal system. This is important for the purpose of market integration, or facilitation of commerce. It is the pragmatic approach, which might be thought likely to succeed.

> The line between what is to be and what can usefully be unified must…be drawn pragmatically and flexibly, not dogmatically or rigidly.[54]

48 Stein (1977: 202).
49 Raff (1999: 15).
50 Lord Bingham (2000: 28).
51 Merryman (1978: 213).
52 Watson (1974: 21).
53 Watson (1978: 321).
54 Markesinis (2000: 31).

3. *A look ahead*

Unification of specified areas of law such as the sale of goods has been successful internationally because of the above arguments. It is not surprising that principles or ideas of law have been slowly recognised as being universal. As an example, principles of continental laws have taken a foothold in common law countries. As England is now part of the EU, such trends will accelerate especially if current attempts in creating a codified European commercial law are successful.[55] A 'flow on effect' can already be observed in continental Europe. Zweigert and Kötz noted:

> In giving his opinion, the national judge is not only entitled to engage with the views of other courts and legal systems; he is also entitled, when applying his own law and naturally giving full weight to its proper construction and development, to take note of the facts that a particular solution conduces to the harmonization of European law. In appropriate cases this argument enables him at the end of the day to adopt the solutions of other legal systems, and it is an argument he should use with increasing frequency as the integration of Europe proceeds.[56]

Moreover, to unify all contract laws of the members of the European Union has become much more than a mere vision. A few years ago, the European Parliament passed a resolution requesting the European organs to start work on a pan-European Contract Law. That was in 1989, repeated a second time in 1994.[57] Although at the beginning the Commission was reluctant, it has now become active. It listed in its communication of 2001[58] the various options available for a further development of the Contract Law in Europe. Based on the opinions which the Commission received, the European Commission published an 'action plan' for a coherent European Contract Law.[59] In this action plan, the Commission provides for the drafting of a so-called 'reference frame' for Contract Law,[60] which should form the basis for further reflection on an optional instrument in the area of European Contract Law. The reference frame is expected to be published by the end of 2007. Several 'think tanks' have taken up work, and the 'soft law codification' in the form of the Principles of European Contract Law

55 Kramer (1996: 137).

56 Zweigert and Kötz (1998: 20).

57 ABl C 158 pp 400–401, Europäische Zeitschrift für Privatrecht 1995, 669.

58 Communication from the Commission to the European Parliament and the Council, A more Coherent European Contract Law, COM(2003) 68 final.

59 Ibid.

60 This common frame of reference should provide for best solutions in terms of common terminology and rules, i.e., the definition of fundamental concepts and abstract terms like 'contract' or 'damage' and of the rules that apply, e.g., in the case of non-performance of contracts.

(1995/1999/2003) shows that the sceptics of a unified, 'Europeanised' contract law are wrong.

III. Unification through the CISG

Considering that the CISG has been placed alongside domestic laws to be used to govern international trade, a twofold approach, at least in theoretical terms, must be considered. The CISG in article 7 implemented a mechanism by which the convention must be interpreted and applied. It also describes the steps to be taken in case a gap within the CISG needs to be filled. As such, article 7 is the process by which the problem of interpretation of the CISG has to be achieved.

However, article 7 also stipulates that the international character of the Convention must be observed. As such, the CISG goes beyond mere harmonisation; it rather demands a uniformity of application and interpretation. Consistent application of the CISG by sovereign states is the goal of unification, but not of harmonisation.

Still, there are views which suggest that unification of international sales laws is and remains a myth. It has been argued that unification has at least a clear goal, whereas harmonisation is indeterminate and less ambitious.[61] Such a view would suggest that uniformity is a tool which at least – because of a clear goal – lends itself to be measured. In other words, the possibility exists to gauge the success of an international convention by objectively determined goals or objectives. Once such goals and objectives are established, acceptance though ratification becomes a possibility.

It is fitting to be reminded that the forerunner of the CISG, Uniform Law on the International Sale of Goods (ULIS), was not a success. It has been argued that ULIS had no chance to succeed from the beginning.[62] It is a reminder that the mere existence of a uniform law does not guarantee its success. Uniformity is not achievable, however arguably harmonisation is. It again highlights the importance of understanding and defining what is meant under unifications of laws. The most important aspect still is the acceptance by its rhetorical community. In other words, the expressed goals and objectives of the international instrument must be acceptable.

Uniform Law on the International Sale of Goods, in effect, faced an unfavourable political situation. The developing countries branded the instrument as favouring the developed countries and as not taking the interests of the developing nations into consideration.[63] The Eastern Block, led by the then Soviet Union, also objected to the Convention. They argued that – in common

61 Boodman (1991: 708).
62 Huber (1979: 414).
63 Huber (1979: 414).

with the underdeveloped and developing nations – they were not adequately represented.[64]

This illustrates that a clear statement of common goals is important. It must be the first step in an analysis of whether the CISG – or any other conventions for that matter – is acceptable. Once the initial step of acceptance has been achieved, the next problem of a uniform application of the international instrument can be studied. 'Uniform words do not always ensure uniform results'[65] because different legal systems may perceive the same words not within the context of the CISG but within the context of their legal traditions. Such a view is flawed, as the goal of the legal instrument, namely uniformity, has not been taken into consideration, The goal of uniformity – as stated previously – is contained in article 7 of the CISG.

Comments such as

> case law interpreting analogous provisions of Article 2 of the Uniform Commercial Code (UCC) may also inform a court where the language of the relevant CISG provisions track that of the UCC.[66]

violate the very rationale behind the creation of the CISG.[67] They suggest that courts apply their own ethnocentric view of legal rules instead of observing the international character of the CISG and exclude domestic jurisprudence from their deliberations. It is the combined view of the international community of courts which will bring about uniformity of application and interpretation. Such views cannot be ignored. This endeavour has been helped by the CISG which uses a simple, non-nation-specific language.[68]

However, this does not mean that all principles must be interpreted autonomously.[69] There is a need to be watchful insofar as terms which are outside the sphere of the CISG must be given the meaning attributable in relation to municipal law. The term 'private international law' is such an example. The term cannot be interpreted uniformly, as it is not directed to an international audience but rather to a domestic one. Jurisdiction, after all, is a domestic issue, as it is

64 However, the telling reason for the failure of ULIS was that the European countries could not agree amongst themselves. An interesting point did emerge. Great Britain – though not unconditionally – ratified ULIS but later found it unnecessary to ratify the CISG. A further point of reluctance amongst sovereign states to ratify ULIS was that work under the auspices of UNCITRAL commenced on the CISG. A working group was established which specifically investigated the need to incorporate countries with different social, economic and legal systems into the drafting process.

65 Baasch-Anderson (1998: 404).

66 *Raw Materials Inc v Manfred Forberich GmbH & Co KG* US District Court of Illinois [http:cisg3.law.pace.edu/cases/040706u1.html].

67 Ferrari (2005: 6).

68 Ferrari (2005: 7).

69 Ferrari (2005: 10).

founded in domestic law and is subject to domestic rules, be they substantive or procedural. However, once the authority of the CISG is established, any further interpretation of substantive issues within the CISG must be referred to the mandate of article 7.

A further point of dispute must be examined. Ferrari again points to the problem of the creation of a 'supranational *stare decisis*'.[70] It is said to be critical because

> it does not take into account the rigid hierarchical structure of the various countries' court systems in which the 'national' *stare decisis* doctrine is embedded.[71]

From a strictly methodological point of view, this is correct, but as the CISG has chosen simple, non-nation-specific language, a pragmatic rather than strict interpretative view is exhibited. Analogically extended, the same pragmatic view must be taken when examining the 'supranational *stare decisis*'. The important aspect, which should not be lost, is that a court has interpreted a particular problem, and decisions of an inferior court of any country must also be treated in the same fashion. The view must be respected and be given persuasive status. Only support from academic writing would enhance its authority. Uniformity is not achieved overnight; it must grow and it must be discovered.

The sheer volume of international decisions – and, with a few exceptions, coming to similar, if not the same conclusions – must be taken as proof that uniformity, at least on a superficial level, is achievable. The mandate of article 7 has been followed and this chapter has shown that it is indeed the cornerstone of the CISG.

It forms the very basis of the argument of this book, whose purpose is to see what effect gap filling has on uniformity of decision making.

70 Ferrrari (2005: 21).
71 Ferr ari (2005: 21).

Chapter 3

Unification of sales laws

A discussion

A. Unification of sales laws – a futility or a success

There are views which suggest that unification of international sales laws remains a myth. On the other hand, strong arguments have been advanced that unification has at least a clear goal, whereas harmonisation is indeterminate and less ambitious.[72] Such a view would suggest that uniformity is a tool and – because of a clear goal – lends itself to be measured. In other words, the possibility exists to gauge the success of an international convention by objectively determined goals or objectives. Once such goals and objectives are established, acceptance through ratification becomes a possibility, and a conclusion can be drawn whether the CISG or any other convention for that matter has achieved unification in a particular area of law. A clear statement of common goals is important. It must be the first step in an analysis of whether the CISG – or any other conventions for that purpose – is acceptable.

Once the initial step of acceptance has been achieved, the problem of a uniform application of the international instrument can be studied next. The suggestion has been made that the reason for the success of the CISG arguably is that it contains very few provisions that would annoy any particular interest group.[73] The rules allow 'unbounded discretion to the decision-makers who must apply them... and allow decision-makers almost any choice they wish'.[74]

I. Uniform words not to ensure uniform results?

Two problems need to be addressed and understood. First, it has been argued that 'uniform words do not always ensure uniform results'.[75] This should allegedly be so because different legal systems may perceive the same words not within the context of the CISG but within the context of their legal traditions. Such a view is

72 Boodman (1991: 708).
73 Stephan (1999: 774).
74 Stephan (1999: 774).
75 Baasch-Anderson (1998: 404).

flawed. The CISG specifically included an interpretative article into its regime to overcome the problems perceived by many writers. If the interpretative article is ignored or not applied correctly, the goal of the CISG has not been taken into consideration. The goal of uniformity – as stated previously – is contained in article 7 of the CISG.

It is patently wrong to argue that

> a decision-maker must wrestle with the choice between using local law to interpret the CISG and following CISG Article 7(1) admonition to promote 'uniformity' among national interpretations.[76]

There simply is no choice. The CISG takes precedent over national law through the principle of ratification. Ignoring rules within a particular legal instrument is not allowed. The problem of not achieving uniformity is not because the rules within the CISG lack consistency and coherence but because the decision makers cannot lift their feet out of the domestic paddock.

II. Unbounded discretion of domestic courts in interpreting uniform law?

The second point of investigation is whether it is true that the CISG gives unbounded discretion to the decision makers. It is correct to observe that the CISG is not written in nation-specific terminology and relies on general principles. However, these general principles are not new inventions. They are principles which are found in most legal families, such as party autonomy and the sanctity of the contract. It is trite to argue that decision makers have unbounded discretion to apply the CISG. On the contrary, in order to give consistency and uniformity to application, the CISG specifically included two articles, namely articles 7 and 8, to assist in the interpretation of not only the Convention but also of individual contracts.

It is true to say that the rules in the CISG are acceptable to most interest groups. Such a statement does not advance anything new regarding the question of uniformity. Any convention in essence is a compromise position. It must be acceptable to most parties otherwise no agreement can be reached amongst the participants of the drafting process. However it does not follow that because the language and principles of the CISG do not annoy any particular interest group unbound discretion in the application of the CISG[77] is allowed.

A convention which does not include interpretative principles arguably may 'allow decision makers almost any choice they wish'.[78] The reason which could be advanced is that any interpretation in a domestic court – absent other

76 Stephan (1999: 778).
77 See Stephan (1999: 774).
78 See Stephan (1999: 774).

rules – must follow domestic principles. However even such reasoning has never found any favours in most courts. In *Fothergill v Monarch Airlines*[79] the House of Lords decision dealt with the interpretation of the Warsaw Convention on the Liability of Air Carriers. This case is important, as it is the foundation on which courts can base their interpretation of international conventions when the treaty does not include any interpretative articles. Lord Diplock stated:

> It should be interpreted . . . unconstrained by technical rules of English law, or by English legal precedent, but on broad principles of general acceptation. [Furthermore] 'the language . . . has not been chosen by an English draftsman. It is neither couched in the Conventional English legislative idiom nor designed to be construed exclusively by English judges'.[80]

Considering that the CISG contains two interpretative articles namely article 7 and 8 there can be no argument to invoke domestic interpretative methods. Once this is understood close attention can be given to the mandate of the CISG. Article 7 demands a uniform application of the convention. Uniformity surely cannot be achieved by ignoring not only the interpretative mandate but also by advocating unbound discretion in applying the CISG.

However there is a problem which the promoters of the CISG could not overcome. Owing to the political nature, and namely to achieve consensus, some legal problems such as validity of contracts had to be excluded as no agreements could be reached. The CISG specifically states that where there are gaps they must be filled by domestic laws. It has been argued that because a dispute could be resolved by a combination of domestic as well as international laws uniformity is not achieved. This book attempts to show that despite gaps in the CISG uniformity still is achievable.

B. Uniformity or domestic competition?

Before investigating the utility of the CISG as a contributing factor to uniformity of international sales law, the argument that alternative methods are superior should be investigated. Stephan notes:

> . . . it seems hard to shake off a sense that the [CISG] does not seem worth the candle, at least if one wishes substantially to improve the legal environment for international transactions. There must be a better way of doing this.[81]

His main argument is that international instruments either compromise legal certainty or advance the agenda of interest groups.[82] He also suggests that

79 [1980] 2 All E.R. 696.
80 Ibid.
81 Stephan (1999: 780).
82 Stephan (1999: 788).

technocratic law making of international instruments has its own political economy with predictable and unattractive implications.[83]

As far as the advancement of an agenda of an interest group is concerned, that may be perfectly correct for certain conventions, such as in shipping and international banking laws. However, the CISG does not favour any interest groups, since it applies for all sales of goods, irrespective of any industry. Obviously, political aspects have contributed to the drafting of the CISG. However there is not a single human enterprise that is not subject to political aspirations and influences. At least with the CISG, the politics was a shifting one and not dominated by one force. The drafting history clearly indicates that special working groups discussed each article, which then was put before the assembly. It can be argued – and the drafting history confirms it – that countries did form loose alliances but not on a continued basis. Each article in effect was treated differently and had its own political aspects. Shifting alliances can be observed and the conclusion can be reached that in this case the political aspect has been kept to a minimum. It should be remembered that domestic legislation is dominated by one master and a technocratic elite, not an ideal position if justice for all is a goal.

The suggestion is that uniformity is not achievable and certainty and justice is better served by allowing national systems to compete among themselves, therefore bypassing 'international bodies, the professorate and legislatures'.[84] The fact is that each national system has been devised by its own legislatures, the technocratic elite and, in most cases, by law professors. The only difference is that instead of dealing with one system, a business now potentially deals with a number of systems. In the end, the question of justice is never achievable and the question of certainty is a question of who the 'term takers' and the 'term givers' are. The effect is that more time and effort is spent on deciding which competing national system must be chosen instead of keeping the 'eyes on the main game' and knowing that a unified system favouring none will determine all legal issues. Forum shopping becomes a feature again, which uniformity of laws tried to overcome.

Combined with forum shopping the other problem which Stephan acknowledges is that: '[w]e simply do not know enough about how particular legal rules operate in different business environments'.[85] The problem is that a prudent person would like to look before he dives, but diverse legal systems contrary to a unified one do not allow such a 'look' unless the party concerned has legal knowledge to overcome the lack of certainty and has either good connections or the language skills necessary to operate within a domestic system. However, it would be impossible to argue that an investigation of legal systems is cost effective considering that a business may need to deal with diverse legal systems. A uniform system has overcome this particular problem.

83 Stephan (1999: 788).
84 Stephan (1999: 788).
85 Stephan (1999: 791).

It is far from realistic to argue that 'the case for national rather than international experimentation seems unassailable'.[86]

It is also true to argue that a reduction of legal risks is best achieved by choosing a fully developed legal system 'with a long history of fairly consistent and elaborate dispute resolution'.[87] But the question of certainty is not resolved, as any system of law by nature is an evolutionary one and in constant development. One only needs to look at the English rule on subjective intent and whether pre- and post-contractual negotiations can be taken into consideration in the construction of a contract. This issue is certainly not settled, but in the CISG, this is a settled issue. Furthermore, the CISG has now crossed its twenty-fifth anniversary and a fairly consistent and extensive jurisprudence is available to guide judges and arbitrators in their deliberations.

These are only some of the arguments which are either advanced to justify unification or to advocate that the best system to solve international disputes is through competition between legal systems.

The simple fact is that unification is not an answer to the question of how best to solve an international legal dispute. Party autonomy, a general principle not only in the CISG but also in most domestic legal systems, will ultimately dictate which system will be choosen. Parties will structure their legal relationship as they see fit. Whether they choose a unified system or rely on a domestic one is ultimately left to the parties concerned. What is important is that at least a system is offered which is uniform. Unification is not to be measured by whether the laws improve what existed before but rather by the availability of a system which is not dependant on domestic rules. In other words a system that is global and, hence, can aspire to be uniform is more useful even if its rules are in places approximations and perhaps need clarifications by judges and arbitrators.

This book therefore is not concerned with which alternative is superior to an international instrument such as the CISG but rather with how successful the CISG has been to able to lay claim to be a uniform international sales law. The question is 'what are we aiming for?'

86 Stephan (1999: 793).
87 Stephan (1999: 792).

Chapter 4

Article 7 CISG

The tool to unified sales laws?

A. Tensions between international legal order and various domestic systems

Some general points need to be made at the outset. If domestic laws of obligation are consulted, it becomes obvious that many of them have existed for decades, even for centuries.[88] Now, to change domestic law only requires an act of parliament. International laws, on the other hand, are much harder to change. It requires a diplomatic conference to convene and approve of the changes. The real challenge is whether all states will accede to the amended convention or not and whether they see it only as a way out of an international obligation. Amendment of the CISG is not perceived to be necessary anyway. Honnold notes succinctly that the CISG

> ... must be read and applied in a manner that permits it to grow and adapt to novel circumstances and changing times.[89]

One of the important tools for responding to changing circumstances is the fact that the language of the CISG is devoid of domestic connotations and describes contractual events in simple plain language. Rabel noted already in 1952 that one of the gains of an international sales law is to avoid 'the awesome relics of the dead past that populate in amazing multitude the older codifications of sales laws'.[90] Honnold has pointed out that today, outdated formulae still complicate domestic sales law.[91] He went on to argue:

> One may delight in legal antiques and in the patina of ingenious circumlocutions that have had to substitute for fundamental reform but these

88 Honnold (1999: 16).
89 Honnold (1999: 16).
90 Rabel (1952: 61).
91 Honnold (1999: 22).

aesthetic values may not be appreciated by a modern merchant and, more especially, by his trading partner from a different legal tradition.[92]

It is not surprising, therefore, that tensions exist between the international legal order and the various domestic systems, which the CISG attempts to replace.[93]

B. Eliminating municipal divergences

Language or the vocabulary is only one part, though an important one, in the definition of the content and values of a uniform law. Kastely, in defining the coherence of the CISG, notes:

> ... the most fundamental [of the values] is the conception of actors under the Convention as different in background and circumstances, yet entitled to equal treatment and respect.[94]

The content and values, specifically those in article 7, are neatly encapsulated by the Romanian delegate to the drafting conference. The delegate succinctly alluded to the values Kastely later elaborated on. He noted in particular:

> ... [i]t was necessary to establish rules that would facilitate commercial transactions on the basis of respect for sovereignty and national independence, non-intervention in the domestic affairs of States and mutual benefit.[95]

Implied in the comments by most delegates was the understanding that uniformisation can only be achieved and hence cater to the needs of the international community by eliminating municipal divergences, which are perceived as obstacles to the necessary growth of international commercial exchange.[96]

Having established a rule of law does not give life to a body of law. Without an audience or a community, such laws remain pure abstractions. Kastely points out that a community has been formed, albeit a rhetorical one. She notes:

> [t]he text of the Convention seeks to establish ... a rhetorical community in which its readers first assent to the language and values of the text itself and then use the language and values to inform their relations with one another.[97]

92 Honnold (1999: 22).
93 Hartnell (1993: 1).
94 Kastely (1988: 594).
95 1 Year Book (1970) UNCITRAL (Doc. a/CN 9/SER A/1970: 54).
96 Marquis (2005: 51).
97 Kastely (1988: 577).

C. The method of interpretation in the CISG

I. Article 7 of the convention

So far, the underpinning values and aspirations of the CISG have been noted as far as necessary for the purpose of this book. However, of importance is the next step, namely to clearly delineate the general principles embodying the values of the convention.

Therefore, besides the choice of language and audience, the most important provision in the CISG – which has been duplicated in many other conventions – is the introduction of an interpretation section. This is a point that has been made repeatedly above but cannot be understated, as it is of paramount importance in achieving uniformity. Such sections have been lacking in earlier treaties and the method of interpretation was left to the Vienna Convention on the Law of Treaties, mainly § 3 and specifically article 31(1).[98] The problem is that the Vienna Convention on the Law of Treaties does not have retrospective force.

Article 7 paints a broad picture that forms the basis for the application of the CISG in a uniform fashion. Several key criteria or standards are stated in article 7. Article 7(1) contains broad principles of application, such as the promotion of uniformity of interpretation, by having regard to its international character and the observance of good faith in international trade.

As far as the goal of uniformity is concerned, article 7(2) is more significant. It concerns the filling of gaps that – as seen later in the book – can give rise to interpretative problems, which have a negative influence on uniformity. Importantly article 7(2) is not only descriptive; of consequence is also what the article does not say.[99] It does not encourage courts to refer to their own law, to approach the CISG in an ethnocentric fashion. Domestic law can only be used as the law of last resort after a rigorous and 'systematic filtering of the various Articles to discern the underlying values of the convention'.[100]

II. Interpreting uniform law

It would be of value to briefly analyse law making in general. An important point needs to be made here. Domestic laws, according to Schwartz and Scott,[101] operate within three models. The premise is that the legislature is comprised of a technocratic elite.

Model 1 is described as the objective, bright line rule. This Model is observed when an interest group's power is strong. Model 2, on the other hand, described as an abstract rule, vesting discretion in decision makers, is used when the

98 Art. 31(1): 'A treaty shall be interpreted in good faith in accordance with the ordinary meaning to be given to the terms of the treaty in their context and in the light of its object and purpose.'

99 Bridge (1997: 288).

100 Bridge (1997: 289).

101 Schwartz and Scott (1994).

pressure of interest groups is weak. Model 3 is a combination of the two other models.[102] Conventions, arguably, should fall within one of the three models if the above theory is correct.

The simple fact is that international laws do not fall within the models described above. A three-tiered system operates. Rather, as far as conventions are concerned, the first tier is which of the opinions of the conference delegates will prevail. The second one is whether the whole conference is in agreement with the draft convention. The third tier is the most important aspect, namely the ratification of the convention by nations. Even in the theory developing rules, a domestic model as described above is inapplicable.

D. Predictability and choice of law

The question of predictability in international trade is intrinsically connected to the question of choice of law.

Unless a convention has become part of the legal system of the states in which the parties have their respective places of business and therefore is to be applied to the contract, the applicable law for at least one party will be a foreign one. The problem is accentuated if a term of a contract calls for the application of a law that is a foreign law for both parties (i.e., a Russian and a Brazilian party agree on Swiss law). This does not mean that the application of a foreign law is necessarily a problem. In *Tolofson v Jensen*,[103] the court applied foreign law rather than the law of the forum for the reasons that:

> the court takes jurisdiction not to administer local law, but for the convenience of litigants, with a view to responding to modern mobility and the needs of a world or national economic order.[104]

Understandably, however, the application of foreign law is always fraught with danger as outcomes are rarely consistent especially in the common law systems where expert witnesses are used to prove the foreign law. A study of 40 American decisions showed that in 36 cases the foreign law was either wrongly applied or the result was highly doubtful.[105] A further problem arises when the foreign law has close links to procedural laws or specific institutions of the foreign country. Then an adjustment to the laws of the forum is difficult, if not nearly impossible. As an example, continental courts find it difficult to apply or understand common law rules based on equity, such as trust and specific performance, and the application of the French rule of *astreinte* is equally difficult.[106] Common law

102 Schwartz and Scott (1994: 605).
103 Canadian Supreme Court [1994] 3 S.C.R 1022.
104 Canadian Supreme Court [1994] 3 S.C.R 1070.
105 Lando (2003: 126 fn 7).
106 Lando (2003: 126 fn 7).

countries find it difficult to understand not only the principle of good faith but also that subjective intent can be used to ascertain the terms of a contract.

There is always a hidden agenda or even antagonism between courts and foreign laws, so covert techniques are often used to secure an outcome that is palatable to the court. It is, therefore, not surprising that the drafters of the CISG attempted to overcome the diversity of municipal laws that pose a serious obstacle to the free exchange of goods.[107] The important function of the CISG, as noted previously, is to overcome the need to resort to the conflict of laws rule, as in effect the same result would be achieved within the four corners of the CISG.

The 'four corner'-approach refers to the four steps to be taken in order to investigate by what law a particular question is governed. First, the express clauses of a contract must be referred to. Second, if judges and arbitrators are unable to resolve the conflict, a reference to domestic law needs to determine the applicable law. Such a reference may lead to the application of unified international law such as the CISG. Third, if the CISG is the law governing a contract, its gaps need to be filled by the applicable domestic law. The fourth criterion is that the interpretation of the CISG must be uniform (article 7) and must avoid any reference to domestic principles and laws.

A further point needs to be made in relation to the issue of fairness and certainty, which is always a point of debate between various legal systems. The underpinning theory of the conventions is that:

> The CISG does not set out its stall in favour of the principle of contractual certainty, which is almost invariably to be purchased at the cost of some flexibility and fairness in the instant case.[108]

The point is that the CISG, being a uniform law, offers the certainty of an a-national application of a law, that does not favour any of the parties. Hence, certainty in the application of the substantive law has been achieved and conflict of laws and the application of foreign laws has diminished substantially. As such, not only certainty but also fairness has been achieved.

E. Domestic law and international business aspirations

I. The inevitable incompleteness of the CISG

The key to the success of the CISG in achieving uniformity is the emergence of an international jurisprudence. To argue that uniformity has been achieved, however, would be an overstatement of facts. In Honnold's words,

> [w]e cannot expect perfect uniformity in applying the Convention – or, for that matter, any other statute. But we can look forward to international

107 Hartnell (1993: 3).
108 Bridge (1997: 290).

> commercial law that is more helpful and predictable than the present Babel of competing systems.[109]

Unfortunately, the CISG is not a complete statement of sales laws. By necessity not all participants at the Diplomatic Conference could agree on all points and compromises had to be made. On certain aspects such as consumer contracts, compromises could not be found and these are excluded pursuant to article 2. The fragmentary nature of the CISG leaves no option but to address the issue of its being inevitably incomplete. Article 7(2) has recognised that there are gaps within the Convention which need filling and, at least indirectly, it clarifies the relationship between the CISG and domestic law.[110]

II. Gaps 'intra' and 'praeter legem'

In order to understand the problem of gap filling, the most important features of the CISG need to be understood. First of all – and this is an obvious point – the CISG only applies in countries that have ratified the Convention or where the contract calls for the CISG as the governing law. Hence, the Convention sits side by side with domestic laws governing the sale of goods. A further point is that the Convention takes precedence over any domestic legislation because the CISG is self-inclusive. However, there is room pursuant to article 6 to either exclude the Convention as a whole or in part if the parties so desire. The effect is that any express terms of the contract will take precedence over the mandate of the CISG. In this context, a problem may arise, namely whether an implied exclusion pursuant to article 6 is possible. This matter will be discussed in Chapter 5.

Invariably, there has to be a boundary between the application of the Convention and the use of domestic law. Article 7(2) states:

> Questions concerning matters governed by this Convention which are not expressly settled in it are to be settled in conformity with the general principles on which it is based or, in the absence of such principles, in conformity with the law applicable by virtue of the rules of private international law.

Exponents of the 'plain language' approach to interpretation could argue that the legislators inserted this language in their text because they intended to have it only apply to certain situations. In effect, it cannot be denied that article 7(2) describes the existence of gaps within the CISG. There are two 'types' of gaps, internal and external gaps. For the purpose of this book, matters that have been excluded from the CISG are termed external gaps or gaps '*intra legem*'. Matters that need settling in accordance with general principles, that is, matters governed by the Convention but not expressly settled are internal gaps or gaps '*praeter legem*'.

109 Honnold (1988: 211–212).
110 Enderlein and Maskow (1992: 57).

The principle of uniformity demands that the use of domestic law is restricted to situations specifically stipulated by the CISG, that is, the filling of external gaps. Rabel already took such a position in 1935 when he discussed the draft of the Uniform Sales Law of 1935.[111] At first glance, there appears to be no problem with the application of domestic laws to settle external gaps.

III. External gaps

1. External gaps – the 'grey area'

A further distinction should be made. External gaps can be divided into two categories. The first group deals with matters that the CISG specifically excludes, such as consumer contracts pursuant to article 2. The second category refers to matters on which the CISG is silent, such as the choice of law. Diedrich uses the terminology of obvious and hidden gaps ('*offensichtliche*' and '*versteckte Regelungslücke*').[112]

The significance of such an observation is twofold. In the first place, obvious gaps delineate external gaps, whereas gaps on which the CISG is silent do not automatically point to an external gap. '*Versteckte Regelungslücke*' should primarily be treated as an internal gap and the method of applying general principles to fill such a gap should be applied. Only when that method does not yield a result will it become clear that the gap is actually an external gap.

Second, in relation to external gaps, where the CISG is silent, article 7 cannot be invoked, as there is no provision that needs interpreting. It must be understood that this only comes into force after the application of general principles yields no result. However, where the external gap is indicated by the CISG a provision or principle needs to be invoked, which requires interpretation. In such an event, the inevitable setting of limits between using principles or provisions within the Convention and the use of domestic law depends on how hard we look for the inclusion of the CISG. This problem will be discussed in the next chapter in detail.

The problem of setting the boundary between obvious and hidden gaps is contained in article 7(2) itself. This points to two critical variables. First, there are 'matters governed by this Convention' and, second, unclear matters that need to be settled in conformity 'with general principles'. The interpretation given to the above is different depending on where the focus is directed to. If the important part is 'matters governed by this Convention', general principles become secondary and are subsumed as long as the Convention governs a question. If, on the other hand, the focus is on general principles then 'matters governed by this Convention' is subordinate to the general principles. The scope

111 Rabel (1935: 55).
112 Diedrich (1995: 353–354).

of the latter interpretation is narrower than the first. A principle is assumed to exist on all matters governed by the CISG. But if there is no 'general principle', a court would need to consult domestic law. Honnold has found an important alternative to domestic law by applying article 9 of the CISG. This suggests that the parties are bound by usage which they have established between themselves. In addition, international trade use, which is widely known and observed by parties, also becomes part of a contract. Thus, article 9 together with article 6 not only supplements the Convention but also, in case of conflict, supersedes the Convention's provisions.[113]

2. *Applying 'general principles' to external gaps*

It is regularly suggested that even if the legal issue is covered by, or exempt from the CISG, domestic law must be used if general principles are lacking.[114] According to that view, general principles are the only point of reference, not the existence of a legal issue. Such a view is possible if we read that 'in the absence of such principles' domestic law can be consulted. In other words, if principles are absent irrespective of whatever is in the CISG, domestic law must be applied.

Arguably, article 7(2) does not lead courts and tribunals to such a conclusion. The CISG specifically alerts interpreters to matters covered and not covered in the Convention. If a legal issue is covered by the Convention then the answer to interpretation must be found within the CISG. Broadly speaking, if the gap pertains to 'the formation of the contract of sale and the rights and obligations of the seller and the buyer',[115] the Convention is applicable. This is supported by the mandate of article 7(1), which demands uniformity in the application of the CISG. It is the discovery of gaps through the application of principles that is supported by the CISG and not the decision whether principles are absent. The mechanism required to fulfil the mandate of article 7(2) therefore is how to fill gaps, and not how to discover principles. The Dutch Supreme Court delivered a judgment, which illustrates the point that a principle covered within the CISG must be resolved without recourse to domestic laws. The question was whether standard terms applied, which contained an exemption clause. The Belgian buyer attempted to rely on the Rome Convention on the Law Applicable to Contractual Obligations namely article 8(2) which would have been favourable to the buyer. The court relied on article 7(2) of the CISG and found that there was no gap because the problem in essence was one of contract formation which was governed by the CISG and therefore rejected the buyer's arguments. 'The *Gran Canaria Tomatoes* case shows that Article 7(2) CISG not only may pre-empt

113 Enderlein and Maskow (1992: 57).
114 Magnus (1989: 118).
115 Enderlein and Maskow (1992: 58).

domestic rules regarding [in this case] general conditions but also protective conflict rules.'[116]

The question is how to develop a mechanism to cover gaps. One approach, which has been advanced, is the 'true code' methodology.[117] In brief, there are no gaps in a 'true code', as a code is a

> Legislative enactment which entirely pre-empts the field and which is assumed to carry within it the answers to all possible questions: thus when a court comes to a gap or an unforeseen situation, its duty is to find, by extrapolation and analogy, a solution consistent with the policy of the codifying law.[118]

The 'true code' relies on an understanding by the interpreter of the policy contained in the code. The CISG expressly stipulates these policies in article 7. The difficulty in applying the 'true code' is that the general principles must be discovered uniformly. If general principles were to be discovered uniformly, and recognised as such, the 'true code method' would serve its purpose. Many common law countries would find such a method unfamiliar and the danger is to apply domestic law instead of filling the internal gap with the help of general principles. Happ alluded to an interesting philosophical distinction in the choice of a methodology of gap filling. He points out that the method to be chosen is a secondary issue. The real question is which method achieves the aim of article 7(1), namely a uniform application of the CISG.[119] This appears to be a circular argument but it highlights the importance that uniformity of interpretation and application of the CISG is the most important consideration. Everything else is subordinate.

F. The mechanism of gap filling

I. *Drafting history of article 7 CISG*

Before attempting to define and clarify the mechanism of gap filling, there is one important aspect of the history of article 7 to be considered. The vote to approve article 7 was 17 in favour, 14 against with 11 abstentions.[120] This shows that the article contains contentious and difficult issues. It also raises another point: how valuable is it to consult the legislative history of article 7(2)? The vote suggests that there were more people who disliked the article than those who liked it. Such a view gives a better insight than the fact that more people voted in favour of the article than against it.

116 De Ly (2005b: 6).
117 Hillman (1997: 2).
118 Hillman (1997: 2).
119 Happ (1997: 379).
120 Hillman (1995: 24).

The conclusion is that the *travaux préparatoires* must be treated with utmost caution. In *Fothergill v Monarch Airlines*[121] and in the Vienna Convention on the Law of Treaties it has been established that history is only of importance if it reflects a general view of the participants. In such a case, the views take on a function of persuasive precedent. However, in this case, can it be said that the views expressed in the legislative history are a general view? There certainly must be doubts cast on such assumptions. Without clear and authoritative historical guidelines courts must take recourse to academic writings. Yet care must be taken that academic reasoning does not displace a practical achievable view important in the establishment of a uniform international law. Courts and tribunals do not aspire to reach a perfect solution. They contend with a practical outcome.

II. The mandate of article 7(1), (2) CISG

With this in mind, it is important not to lose sight of the mandate of article 7(1). This article sets the stage for the interpretation by promoting a uniform approach using good faith and the international character of the convention. In other words, article 7(1) defines the purpose and the principle of interpretation and is applied to the Convention as a whole. As such, it also includes article 7(2), which goes beyond the 'big picture' and settles the problems of gap filling.

It is also important to understand that the mandate of the CISG is to 'look for a solution', which is not only restricted to interpretation but extends to solving a problem. The problem in this chapter is to find out how gap filling is achieved and, because of the autonomous mandate of interpretation, to explain and understand its relationship with domestic law. The solution to the interpretation of article 7(2) must be found within the 'four corners' of the CISG.

To restate, article 7(2) describes two situations where gap filling is needed. First, if the matter is governed by the Convention but not expressly settled, then a gap must be filled in conformity with general principles on which it is based. Second, if the matter is not covered then the gap must be filled taking domestic law into consideration. There are two reasons why a matter may not be covered by the Convention. First and most obviously, it has been specifically excluded from the sphere of application by the CISG itself, such as validity in article 4. Second, changes in business methods will lead to gaps.

III. A German trilogy of cases

1. Three times article 7 – three different results

The problem of applying article 7(2) can be illustrated through a 'trilogy' of German decisions. The dispute commenced in the Landgericht[122] and via the

121 [1980] 2 All E.R. 696.

122 Landgericht Heidelberg, 2. Kammer fur Handelsachen, 2 October 1996, O 37/96 KfH II [http://cisgw3.law.pace.edu/cases/961002g.1.html] last update 16 April 2001.

Oberlandesgericht[123] was finally settled on appeal in the Bundesgerichtshof.[124] The central question hinged on the interpretation of 'reasonable time' pursuant to article 39(2). In brief, a German seller delivered surface-protective film to an Austrian buyer. The buyer did not test the film on delivery. When he used the product, he found that it left a residue of glue on the surface. The buyer notified the seller the next day of the problem but this notice was given 24 days after the film had been delivered.

As 'reasonable time' is not defined in the CISG, a gap exists, which needs filling. It has been recognised that 'reasonableness' is a general principle of the CISG, hence, at first glance, gap filling pursuant to article 7(2) should be achievable. The Landgericht pointed to the fact that article 39 does not set a time in which notice as to defects must be given to the seller. The court also pointed out that a fixed time limit is alien to many domestic systems except Italy, which sets a time limit of 8 days.[125] The court used doctrinal evidence to come to the conclusion that the term 'reasonable' was a compromise in the drawing up of the Convention.[126] It must be assumed that the court concluded that *travaux préparatoires* were of no help except to indicate that the final article 39 was more 'buyer friendly' than its predecessor. This led the court to the conclusion that one month was appropriate with the proviso that depending on circumstances the period can be shorter.[127]

The Oberlandesgericht reversed the decision on appeal on the grounds that the notification of the lack of conformity was untimely. They argued that the time starts when the lack of conformity 'could' have been discovered, not 'when' it was discovered.[128] Further, the buyer ought to have undertaken a trial run to ascertain whether the goods conformed to the desired quality. The court also examined a matter which the lower court did not take into consideration, namely the negotiations between the parties in relation to the fixing of the defects. The court came to the conclusion that the negotiations pursuant to article 7(1) were in good faith and so did not impinge on the breach of article 39.[129]

The German Federal Court reversed that decision again but unfortunately made no comment on the decisions given in relation to 'reasonable time' by the lower court. The court found that the most important fact were the negotiations both parties had in relation to the fixing of damages. It also found that the fact of entering into negotiation amounts to implicitly waiving the right to rely on articles 38 and 39.[130] Unfortunately, the court did not expressly rely on article 7 – as

123 Oberlandesgericht Karlsruhe, 1. Zivilsenat, 25 June 1997, 1 U 280/96 [http://www.jura.uni-freiburg.de/ipr1/cisg/urteile/text/263.html].

124 Bundesgerichtshof, VIII. Zivilsenat, 25 November 1998, VIII ZR 259/97 [http://cisgw3.law.pace.edu/cases/981122225g1.html] last update 25 October 2000.

125 Art. 1495(1) Codice Civile.

126 Landgericht Heidelberg, above fn 122.

127 Landgericht Heidelberg, above fn 122.

128 Oberlandesgericht Karlsruhe, above fn 123.

129 Oberlandesgericht Karlsruhe, above fn 123.

130 Bundesgerichtshof, above fn 124.

the previous court did for the wrong reasons – to substantiate the decision. It certainly is a breach of good faith that a seller can enter into negotiations to fix a defect and then turn around and deny the buyer remedies, which he would have had had he not negotiated in the first instance. In sum, the court did reach the correct conclusion unfortunately without the appropriate explanations. By contrast, Bonell as the sole arbitrator in an almost identical case held that the seller was not permitted to raise the defence of late notice pursuant to article 39 and the general principle of good faith was used to fill the gap.[131]

2. *Conclusions*

What conclusions can be drawn from the above? It certainly showed that a gap exists, which needs filling, however neither of the courts indicated what method they used to fill the gap, as they did not refer to article 7(2). The difference between the court of first instance and the first appeal merely indicated a more sophisticated line of reasoning in determining a 'reasonable time'. The lower court did take a simple approach but it did take note of scholarly writings. The attempt was made to find a solution within the 'four corners' of the CISG, which shows that the hypothesis of this thesis is still affirmed. The Oberlandesgericht Karlsruhe showed a better insight by recognising that good faith pursuant to article 7(1) was also applicable. The court, however, despite good intentions, showed a lack of understanding by not taking a holistic approach to the application of good faith. In the end, the German Federal Court arrived at the correct decision in relation to the case. Unfortunately, however, it did not re-examine the gap-filling requirement and did not refer to the reasons of good faith to come to its conclusion.

The above 'trilogy' also confirms the importance of selecting persuasive precedent from reported international jurisprudence. Only decisions of the highest court in any court hierarchy should be confidently used to create persuasive precedent. However decisions of lower courts should not be entirely ignored as they give an invaluable insight into the persuasiveness of the CISG within a domestic system. The above case shows that all levels of the German court hierarchy did show a level of sophistication and knowledge in the application of the CISG.

In sum, it can be argued that it was not obvious whether the courts engaged in gap filling. They did not indicate clearly the use of the general principles nor did they show a method of applying article 7(2). It must be said that the courts did come to a conclusion but only by interpreting words within the relevant articles. The above discussion shows how difficult it is to recognise gaps in an appropriate manner in all circumstances. Courts may feel that interpretation rather than gap filling will bring about a solution to a dispute.

131 Vienna Arbitration proceeding, SCH-4318, 15 June 1994. [http://cisg3.law.pace.edu/cases/940615a4.html] update 8 September 1999.

Chapter 5

Conflict of laws

Is uniformity possible?

A. Controversies in the application of the CISG

Unification, as shown in previous chapters, is an elusive goal. It is a myth that the mere existence of a unified document, such as the CISG or the UNIDROIT Principles, guarantee unification in sales and contract law, respectively. To expect a full unification would be a utopian enterprise, as domestic public policy and the desire to protect a particular class of people will never allow a full unification to take place. However, what can be said is that unification on the main issues of contractual laws is achievable. Not only is it achievable, it already has happened. The necessity for unification of laws is evidenced by the fact that domestic law is inadequate as a framework in dealing with international commercial transactions. As to international commercial sales, every opportunity must be seized to take recourse to the CISG, and any recourse to domestic law must only be the last resort. In other words, an interpretation of the CISG must be within its four corners.

There are, in essence, three levels of the legal process, which create – in some instances – an irreconcilable nationalisation of a problem which is in contrast to the mandate of uniformity. The process is started by the plaintiff applying to a particular jurisdiction to have the case adjudicated. Unfortunately, this in turn will trigger the application of a domestic determination of the particular substantive law through the conflict of laws rules.

> The domestic character of these rules stands in sharp contrast to the international or transnational character and quality of the cases that are subject to these rules. The inherent conflict has been rightly characterized as the 'inveterate evil of private international law'.[132]

Once the applicable domestic law has been ascertained, the question of whether the CISG is part of that body of law and, hence, applicable needs to be determined. Arguably, therefore, the conflict between international and domestic laws 'is played out each time a judge or arbitrator has to decide whether an issue falls

132 Berger (1999: 9).

within the scope of the Convention'.[133] This is not the only point where a conflict can potentially emerge; many judges and arbitrators approach a unified document, such as the CISG, in an ethnocentric manner. They look at the wording, and because it looks familiar, the assumption is made that domestic jurisprudence can be used to determine the matter. However, the method of construction is stipulated in the CISG in articles 7 and 8 and domestic rules as to interpretation cannot be used. The latest example which illustrates this point is *Raw Materials Inc v Manfred Forberich GmbH*.[134] This case was nominated as the worst CISG decision in 25 years.[135] It is rather disturbing that, despite ample academic writing, a court in 2004 still can maintain that '…in applying Article 79 of the CISG, the court will use as a guide case law interpreting a similar provision of article 2-615 of the UCC'.[136] This was in response to the plaintiff's assertion that '[w]hile no American court has specifically interpreted or applied Article 79 of the CISG, case law interpreting the UCC [provides] guidance for interpreting the CISG article 79'.[137] The correct approach would have been to consult international case law on the CISG, which, in this case, consisted of 27 reported cases.[138]

It is encouraging to note that domestic courts have started to understand that uniformity in the interpretation of international law is an important feature, which contributes towards certainty and predictability in international trade. Especially in the area of transplantation – in this case the Warsaw Convention – the courts have recognised that:

> [a] decision must be reached by this court with close attention to any relevant developments of international law, including decisions of the municipal courts of other states parties.[139]

The Australian High Court went even further and clearly stated that 'no differentiation could be drawn on the basis that it was not obligatory for Australia to apply the language of the Warsaw Convention to domestic carriage by air within Australia'.[140]

The mere fact that the Warsaw convention was transplanted into Australian domestic law was sufficient for the High Court to abandon ethnocentric interpretation in favour of an international one.

Similarly, the German Bundesgerichtshof rejected the application of national limitation periods rules under the Warsaw Convention because the convention

133 Hartnell (1993: 7).
134 [http:cisg3.law.pace.edu/cases/040706u1.html].
135 See Lookofsky and Flechtner (2005: 199).
136 *Raw Materials Inc v Manfred Forberich GmbH & Co KG* US District Court of Illinois [http:cisg3.law.pace.edu/cases/040706u1.html].
137 *Raw Materials Inc v Manfred Forberich GmbH & Co KG* US District court of Illinois [http: cisg3.law.pace.edu/cases/040706u1.html].
138 See Zeller (2005: 177).
139 *Air Link Pty Limited v Paterson* [2005] HCA 39 (10 August 2005) 40.
140 *Air Link Pty Limited v Paterson* [2005] HCA 39 (10 August 2005) 49.

itself provides for a preclusion period. It held that the preclusion period in the Warsaw Convention has the same function as a limitation period and does, therefore, functionally replace it. Therefore, it leaves no space for the application of national law.[141]

To go one step further, even if international, uniform law has not been transplanted, its mere existence has been reason enough to align domestic law with the uniform model. As an example, several court decisions and arbitral awards have interpreted domestic commercial law provisions in light of the corresponding provisions of the Principles of European Contract Law and the UNIDROIT Principles, although the latter have no legal basis in domestic law.[142]

Considering that the CISG is not a transplantation, but a ratification of a treaty, no excuse or reason not to adopt an international interpretation can be advanced. Hopefully, the approach of those recent developments in case law dealing with international conventions and sets of rules, respectively, will be followed to resolve two specific problems that need to be addressed within the framework of the CISG. First, the appropriate forum or jurisdiction must be determined, and second, the relevant substantive law needs to be applied. It is a settled law that the applicable jurisdiction must be resolved first; only then can a court inquire which is the applicable law.

B. Issues of application of the CISG

I. Introduction

The question of jurisdiction is an interesting problem. It is, in essence, a question of procedural law. After all, it merely determines whether a court intends to allow a party the right to choose a forum. Still, it is 'the opening shot' to determine the applicable law – if there is no express clause in the contract – because every forum will apply its own conflict of laws rules.

> Within the internal legal order of a State it raises the problem of interaction between the conventions' rules on the sphere of application of the uniform substantive law and the *lex fori* conflict-of-laws rule.[143]

141 Bundesgerichtshof, decision of 24 March 2005 – I ZR 196/02, *Internationales Wirtschaftsrecht* (= Recht der Internationalen Wirtschaft) 2005, 625.

142 See ICC Award No. 8486, Clunet 1998, 10478, with note Y. Derains, 1050 et seq., construing the provision on force majeure of the Dutch Civil Code in light of the UNIDROIT Principles; see also on this award Berger (2001: 31 *et seq*); see furthermore H. Wiedemann's case review of the German Bundesgerichtshof, 26 September 1997, in 1998 Juristenzeitung 1173 *et seq*; an interesting dogmatic approach has been provided by Kramer (1999: 82): the reference in the last sentence of the Preamble of the UNIDROIT Principles to 'national and international legislators' should be construed in a functional manner so as to encompass domestic judges who develop the law 'like legislators' under Art. 1(2) Swiss Civil Code. On the discussion under the German Civil Code, see the contributions in Basedow (ed) (2000).

143 Conetti (1986: 387).

The determination of the conflict of laws rule is not entirely within the mandate of the CISG. To complicate the matter, the CISG includes a system of reservations which allow contracting states to exclude article 1(1)(b).[144] It must be noted that only five states have declared a reservation under article 95, namely China, Singapore, the Czech Republic, Slovakia, and the USA. Interestingly enough, Bridge states that:

> the only plausible ground for the Article 95 reservation is an altruistic regards for the integrity of the CISG as though the 'Venus de Milo' is worthless without its arms... [and] the prospect of a somewhat chauvinistic preference for a state's own legal system hoves into sight.[145]

However, upon closer examination the reasons for the various states to enter an article 95 reservation are varied and not as simple as Bridge suggests. The *travaux préparatoires* clearly explain that the original reservation was meant to be used by socialist countries which had special legislation governing contracts with foreign parties, like the former Soviet Union, the Czech Republic and, until 1999, China.[146] The USA, on the other hand, was concerned with clarity of the choice of law, and second, they were worried that US law would be displaced more often than foreign law.[147] Singapore, on the other hand, was concerned that the parties to a contract may unwittingly end up with the CISG as their law when they intended that Singapore domestic law should apply.[148] Not surprisingly, Bell argues that an article 95 reservation only leads to confusion, complicated conflict of laws problems, and forum shopping. He argues that for these and other policy reasons, Singapore should withdraw its reservation and stop protecting incompetent lawyers who still do not understand that Singapore is a party to the CISG.[149]

The wording of article 95 does not make it entirely clear how far reaching the reservation is: is only the state which has made a reservation not bound by article 1(1)(b), or must also the courts in other states respect the article 95 reservation? For example, is the forum state, whose conflicts of laws rules point to the law of a state that has made a reservation under article 95, bound by the reservation? Germany has answered this question in the affirmative.[150] The interesting point is

144 Art. 95 CISG: 'Any State may declare at the time of the deposit of its instrument of ratification, acceptance, approval or accession that it will not be bound by subparagraph (1)(b) of art. 1 of this Convention.' See thereto, e.g., Oberlandesgericht Düsseldorf (Germany), 2 July 1993, CISG-online 74.

145 Bridge (1997: 293).

146 Bell (2005: 58).

147 Bell (2005: 59).

148 Bell (2005: 61).

149 Bell (2005: 55 ff).

150 See art. 2 of the German 'Gesetz zu dem Übereinkommen der Vereinten Nationen vom 11. April 1980 über Verträge über den internationalen Warenkauf sowie zur Änderung des Gesetzes zu dem Übereinkommen vom 19. Mai 1956 über den Beförderungsvertrag im internationalen Straßengüterverkehr (CMR)', Burgerlieches Gesetzbuch (BGBl) II 586.

how many countries follow the German lead and also do not apply article 1(1)(b) if the choice of law would, for example, lead to the application of US law. It is difficult to imagine a Spanish court being willing to apply the UCC if they could apply the CISG by following their own legal principles (article 1(1)(b)). The wording of article 95 is clear, as it states that 'it' will not be bound – that is, the state making the reservation. Article 92, on the other hand, makes it perfectly clear that any state making a declaration under it is not to be considered a contracting state 'in respect of matters governed by the Part to which the declaration applies'. The problem is that these last minute introductions to the CISG are not conducive to a uniform application of the Convention. To date, only 17 decisions have been made in relation to article 92, and 13 cases in respect of article 95.[151]

The most telling problem is that if one were to follow the position upheld by German law, uniformity of application is being lost. If, as an example, a Japanese seller would chose Singapore law, but the forum was Australia, Australia must observe the reservation made by Singapore (article 95) and hence, Singapore domestic law would need to be applied.

The question in the light of the above discussion would be whether Australia will feel obliged – like Germany – to apply Singaporean domestic law. If, namely, one understood the reservation in article 95 to refer only to the state having made the reservation, the scope of application of the CISG is considerably broader. Foreign forum states would not be bound by the reservation, to the effect that article 1(1)(b) applies. In our example, Singapore being a contracting state, the choice of Singaporean law would lead to the application of the CISG. If, on the other hand, Singapore had been also the forum, the CISG would not have been the governing law. In the end, the conflict of laws rules of a domestic court will decide the issue, which, no doubt, will never lead to a uniform solution to this problem.

For the above reasons, the CISG cannot entirely avoid dealing with private international law rules and problems concerning the internal conflict of laws rules.[152] Generally speaking, in the absence of express terms, there is no single set of gap filling laws specified.[153] The result is that parties are uncertain as to which default rule will apply, to the effect that the whole process of an international transaction has an uncertainty at the beginning.

Conflict rules are not 'tailored to select efficient default rules for international transactions and the institutional problems in structuring them to so do seem insurmountable'.[154] Only a contractual choice of law clause or an international convention would solve this point. However, the domestic choice of laws rule will still decide which municipal law will fill the gaps left open by the CISG

151 See Pace Website.
152 Conetti (1986: 387).
153 Linarelli (2002: 339).
154 Linarelli (2002: 340).

(for which no general principle can be derived). It needs to be remembered that once a country ratified the CISG, it has become part of domestic law. In essence, once a domestic law has been chosen, either by an express term or by the conflict of laws rule, the next step would be to find out whether article 1 of the CISG would apply.[155] If the answer is 'yes', then the CISG will take the position of first choice of applicable law.

Even if the traditional view is taken, namely that the applicable law is the one with which the legal relationship has the closest and real connection, it does not lead necessarily to the application of the 'best law' to resolve a practical matter and, hence, respond to the needs and interests of international commerce.[156]

The problem, which the CISG has not been able to solve and, hence, does not contribute towards certainty is that 'choice of law is a solution only where the parties can at low cost obtain information about the laws of various countries'.[157] This is only applicable in limited situations, where parties have been dealing with the same customers and, hence, should be or are aware of the legal situation of each of the common trading partners. However, the problem still remains that even if certain knowledge has been accumulated, certainty or uniformity in selecting a proper law has not been solved. Simply put, the more knowledgeable party has an advantage in dealing with legal diversity.[158] One fact remains: the uncertainties surrounding the selection of the applicable law make contractual risk management more difficult and transaction costs will increase.[159]

Considering that, in the absence of a choice of law clause, the contract in most cases will be subject to the closest and real connection,[160] some problems may be resolved. However, there is no guarantee that the outcome is a workable one considering the international character of the transactions. As an example, we assume that a Swiss buyer and an Australian seller meet at a trade fair in England. They discuss the option of entering into a contract between the two businesses. Both businesses are traders and they buy pre-ordered goods from many countries. Assuming that this contract calls for the sale of goods, which are warehoused in Italy, many possible solutions can be envisaged. Jurisdiction can be sought in England where the contract was formed, in either Switzerland or Australia where the parties have their place of business, or even in Italy, where the goods are warehoused.

155 A problem in interpretation can already emerge, as the decisive factor in art. 1 is the place of business of the contracting parties. Despite the fact that the place of business is not defined in the CISG, art. 10 will assist a court or tribunal to reach a solution which is dictated by sound practical reasons, not by abstract legal reasoning.

156 Berger (1999: 11).

157 Linarelli (2002: 340).

158 Linarelli (2002: 341).

159 Berger (1999: 12).

160 *Bonython v Commonwealth of Australia* [1951] AC 201, p 219; Rome Convention art. 4(1); Hague Convention 1986 art. 8(1).

The solution to this problem does not lie with the right of a plaintiff to seek the jurisdiction which suits him best, but with the determination of the applicable substantive law because it will contribute to a uniform solution. The CISG in a sense offers the solution to the problem. Most choice of laws rules follow the maxim that the law with the closest connection to the contract is the applicable one. If article 31 and 57(1) are consulted, a general principle can be developed.

II. Conflict of laws

It would be of value to point out again that contract law is based on a consensual exchange and therefore the concept of the default rule plays an important part.[161] This rule fills the gap of an incomplete contract. It is superior to an immutable or mandatory rule as

> [d]efault rules can reduce the costs of contracting whereas immutable rules increase those costs, if preference for legal rules are not homogenous.[162]

A solution to this problem can be supplied by the CISG in the form of a general principle. However, the principle within the CISG must be able to take on the mantle of a conflict of laws rule, which would or could be applied and would displace any domestic law in this area. This would be permissible as the convention is applicable if the mandate of article 1 is adhered to. The necessary determination of the domestic law could be uniformly applied and would not be subject to varied and complicated domestic principles. It is of value to understand that 'unfortunately government officials and contract lawyers are often not very familiar with the principles of private international law'.[163] The result is that parties to a dispute cannot be sure which law a tribunal or court will actually apply. This would give strength to the observation that the CISG within its four corners has a general principle, which could be applied in lieu of a domestic private international law rule. This view is supported by the fact that:

> the essential quality of [a] uniform substantive law is its applicability to those cases specified by the restrictions it sets on its own sphere of application.[164]

Thus, if articles 31 and 57(1) are considered to be restrictions in relation to conflict of laws, they would displace the domestic private international law rules. Such an interpretation would fulfil the intrinsic task of uniformity and therefore

161 Whincop and Keyes (1997: 516).
162 Whincop and Keyes (1997: 516).
163 Volken (1986: 29).
164 Conetti (1986: 329).

provide certainty in international contractual dealings. This is especially so, as the private international law 'amounts to an engine of international discord detracting from the unity of the CISG that courts and arbitrators should only use as a last resort'.[165]

Court decisions and legal literature have stated that article 57(1) makes it possible for a seller to start proceedings against the buyer at the seller's place of business.[166] The combination of a conflict of laws rule which allows for a venue of proceedings at the place of performance together with article 57 has developed to a generally accepted way of determining jurisdiction. Arguably, therefore, article 57(1) contributes to uniformity of law.

It is useful to consider in brief the important features of a conflict of law rule. The court which accepts jurisdiction must not only decide the applicable law but also the system from which this rule is to be drawn. The choice of laws rules are those of the forum, and hence, the governing or substantive law is determined through this process.

English courts have pointed out that the

> proper law of the contract 'is the law which the parties intended to apply'. That intention is objectively ascertained and, if not expressed, will be presumed from the terms of the contract and the relevant surrounding circumstances.[167]

It is, therefore, possible for a court to infer the intention of the parties from the contract and extrinsic material, such as the type of contract or jurisdiction clauses.[168] If article 1(1)(a) applies, the governing or substantive law is the CISG. Once such a determination has been reached, the general principles of the CISG derived from articles 31 or 57(1) can be applied.

It should be made clear that the question is not necessarily which domestic law or forum is the most appropriate one but also which system of law has the closest connection to the dispute. If the system of law is more appropriate, then the form and content of the contract assumes greater importance.

If the content of the contract plays an important role, the CISG, if applicable under article 1, would need to be consulted, as subjective as well as objective consideration would lead to a desired result. The opposite view would be that the place where jurisdiction is sought would be the appropriate forum to determine the substantive law which will solve this issue. However, this would lead to inconsistencies as on the one hand, the choice of law would be determined by looking at objective considerations only, but the subjective issue would subsequently be adjudicated with both subjective as well as objective facts to be

165 Bridge (1997: 285).
166 Ferrari (2002a: 692).
167 *Vita Food Products Incorporated v Unus Shipping Co* [1939] AC 277, p 290.
168 Whincop and Keyes (1997: 519).

considered if the CISG were applicable. Arguably, an inconsistency, perhaps even injustice, could be the result, leave alone any uniformity that could be achieved.

However, the argument as put by the House of Lords in *Cie d'Armament Maritime SA v Cie Tunesienne de Navigtion SA*[169] is that the connection is not between the legal system and the contract itself but rather with the underlying transaction. Such a view would suggest that the place of performance would have a bearing on the underlying transaction. Case law supports this contention. In *Mendelsohn-Zeller Inc v T & C Providores Ltd,*[170] the place of performance was determined to be California because that was the place where the seller was obliged to deliver the goods under a CIF contract. This ruling was confirmed in *Laminex (Aust) Pty Ltd v Coe Manufacturing Co.*[171] Furthermore, courts decided that the place where payment is due is substantially the relevant forum.[172] It appears that courts in Australia have followed the recommendation of the Australian Law Reform Commission. The Commission defined the place as:

> where the party to the contract that is to effect the performance that is characteristic of the contract habitually resides unless the contract has its most real and substantial connection with another place.[173]

Returning to the assertion that articles 31 and 57(1) can be used to extract a general principle that will make a choice of laws irrelevant, it needs to be considered specifically in light of the above conclusions.

Article 31 describes the obligations of the seller whereas article 57(1) deals with the obligations of the buyer. Simply put, article 31 first upholds a possible contractual duty, namely that the seller is obliged to deliver the goods at any particular agreed place. If there is no such obligation, his obligation to deliver goods consists 'in handing the goods over to the first carrier for transmission to the buyer'. This obligation corresponds as close as possible to an INCOTERM FCA contract. The remainder of article 31, in essence, repeats the above as in all other cases the seller is obliged to place the goods 'at the buyer's disposal at the place where the seller had his place of business'. It can be argued that in line with judicial precedent, the closest connection is the seller's place of business. As far as the buyer's obligation is concerned, article 57(1) demands that the price is paid to the seller 'at the seller's place of business'.

In other words, an application of articles 31 and 57(1) leads to the same conclusion, namely that the performance of contractual obligations is due at the seller's place. The same result is dictated by the choice of laws rules in Australia and England. Arguably, therefore, the CISG through a general principle contains

169 [1971] AC 572.
170 [1981] 1 NSWLR 366.
171 [1999] NSWCA 370.
172 See *Olex Focas Pty Ltd v Skodaexport Co Ltd* [1998] 3 VR 380.
173 Australian Law Reform Commission, *Choice of Law*, Report No 58 (1992), p 98.

a choice of law clause and therefore, once the CISG is applicable via article 1, a domestic choice of laws clause cannot be invoked. Such an approach would guarantee uniformity, as the CISG can assist in determining the forum insofar as the place of business or the closest connection to the contract is concerned.[174]

The problem is, however, *whether* article 1 allows such an interpretation. It has been accepted that article 1 has been specifically drafted in order to conform to the rules of private international law. As indicated specifically in article 1(1)(b), the CISG is applicable if the rules of international law of the *lex fori*, by the rules of the closest connection to the contract, point to the application of the law of a contracting state.[175] At this stage, the observation can be made that articles 31 and 57(1) achieve the same result as any court applying common law choice of laws rules. Even if an express choice of law has been made in the contract the problem is that this choice will only be accepted if there is a reasonable link with the contract. However, the problem does arise when no choice has been made. In this case, the default rule would be called into play. As argued previously, the default rule is a general principle of the CISG, and hence, there is no need to invoke a domestic law.

The argument can be advanced that articles 31 and 57 only state a general principle because most other legal systems combine the place of delivery with the place of venue. So, one might say, it is only a matter of fact that the CISG has adopted a rule known to most domestic laws, but it is not enough to constitute a general principle. Such an argument, however, must be rejected. First, the fact that most domestic laws adopted such a rule and this rule is included in the CISG suggests that a uniform rule has been created. Second, and in support of the first contention is the fact that only principles that are universal in nature would be acceptable to the delegates at the UNICTRAL conference. This is basically the foundation on which uniformity has been built. There are very few principles within the CISG which are novel and are not found in most legal systems. Therefore, if the mechanism to discover a general principle is applied articles 31 and 57 do indeed suggest that a conflict of laws rule can be elicited from the CISG.

There is further evidence to be gained to support the above conclusion from the common law. In England, prior to 1990, that is, when the UK acceded to the Rome Convention, two tests were used to determine the applicable law. The first was the ‘closest and most real connection’ test, as adopted in *Bonython v Commonwealth of Australia*,[176] and the second was the test of objective presumed intention.[177] However, the dividing line between the two tests was frequently blurred.[178]

174 Zeller (2002: 326).
175 Borisova (2004).
176 *Bonython v Commonwealth of Australia* [1951] AC 201, p 219.
177 *Lloyd v Guibert* (1865) LR 1 QB 115.
178 Dicey, Morris and Collins (2000: 1197).

Basically, the courts adopted a three-tiered approach. As a first step, they looked for an express choice of law. If such a choice was not made, they looked for an indication of the parties' intention. Only if no such intention was detectable would a court, as a third step, find out with what system of law the contract had its closest connection.[179] In practice, however, the courts moved directly from the first to the third stage because the tests of inferred intention and close connection merged into each other.[180]

Arguably, therefore, the application of article 1(1)(a) of the CISG would lead to the same result, namely to move directly to the determination of the governing law. The fact that both parties live in convention states could infer that the CISG would be the governing law, and furthermore, it also contains articles which determine the real and closest connection to the contract. The result is that the CISG can deliver a default rule which to all intent and purposes is the fallback position and ultimate decision anyway.

III. Applying the law of the seller's state

The CISG, as seen above, will supply at least a default conflict of law rule favouring the law of the seller's state. The goals of uniformity and certainty are general principles which are not only embedded within the CISG but are also aspired goals in many legal systems. However, in international trade uniformity and certainty are of special significance and must be sufficient grounds to pre-empt state contract causes of action.[181] In *Asanta Tech. Inc v PMG-Sierra Inc*, [182] the court made special reference to the problem of the conflict of law issue. Both parties included a choice of law provision into their contracts. The plaintiff buyer from the United States identified the law of the state shown on the buyer's address, the seller from Canada pointed to the laws of British Columbia and the laws of Canada.

The court noted:

> The availability of independent state contract law causes of action would frustrate the goals of uniformity and certainty embraced by the CISG. Allowing such avenues for potential liability would subject contracting parties to different states' laws and the very same ambiguities regarding international contracts that the CISG was designed to avoid. As a consequence, parties to international contracts would be unable to predict the applicable law, and the fundamental purpose of the CISG would be undermined.[183]

The problem is that the court only solved half of the problem. They determined which law was applicable and correctly pointed to the CISG by

179 Dicey, Morris and Collins (2000: 1197).

180 Dicey, Morris and Collins (2000: 1197).

181 Pribetic (2004).

182 United States 27 July 2001 Federal District Court [California] [http://www.cisg.law.pace.edu/cisg/wais/db/cases2/010727u1.html].

183 United states 27 July 2001 Federal District Court [California] [http://www.cisg.law.pace.edu/cisg/wais/db/cases 2/01p 727u1.html].

asserting that 'where a contract for an international sale of goods does not make clear what rule of law applies, the Convention provides uniform rules to govern the question'.[184] However, they neglected to also use the CISG to determine the relevant forum which would have been the seller's country. In *Kling & Freitag GmbH s.r.l. v Societa Reference Laboratory S.r.l.*,[185] the court at least recognised the importance of article 31. The problem was that jurisdiction was sought in Italy but the German seller objected to the jurisdiction and the court, in the first instance, consulted Art. 5(1) of the 1968 Brussels Jurisdiction and Enforcement Convention. The conclusion was that the jurisdiction was vested in the state where the seller had to deliver the goods. Once that was established, the court concluded that the CISG applies and, pursuant to article 31, the place of delivery being Germany, jurisdiction is vested in a German court. This case at least shows that a court was aware that article 31 is useful in determining the jurisdiction and, hence, the conflict of laws rule.

Arguably, articles 31 and 57 contribute to and frame the general principle of a *lex fori conventionis*, which should be applied to increase uniformity and certainty.

There are several treaties that require courts to apply the rule as embodied in the CISG, which suggests that uniformity on a treaty level is achievable. There are, basically, three treaties and one (regulation proposal) which are noteworthy, namely the 1955 Hague Convention, the 1986 Hague Convention, and the 1980 Rome Convention.

The 1955 Hague Convention on the Law Applicable to International Sales of Goods came into force in 1964.[186] Article 3 can be relied upon if the parties have not made an express choice of the governing law. The article states that the sales

> shall be governed by the domestic law of the country in which the vendor has his habitual residence at the time when he receives the order.

As in the majority of cases, if the buyer's order is received in the seller's country, it can be taken that the law of the seller's country governs the transaction.[187] The 1986 Hague Convention was designed to replace the 1955 Convention but has not yet received enough ratification to come into force.[188] It provides in article 8(1) that 'the contract is governed by the law of the state where the seller has his place of business at the time of the conclusion of the contract'.

The 1980 Rome Convention, in effect, does also provide the rule that the contract shall be governed by the law of the seller.[189] This is contained in articles 4(1) and (2). The Rome Convention aligned itself with the 'most closely connected'

184 United states 27 July 2001 Federal District Court [California] [http://www.cisg.law.pace.edu/cisg/wais/db/cases 2/01p 727u1.html].

185 [http://www.unilex.info/case].

186 22 Dec. 1986, 24 I.L.M. 1575.

187 Mather (2001: 183).

188 Mather (2001: 183).

189 Mather (2001: 184).

principle and not with the open-ended 'most significant relationship analysis'.[190] The Proposal for transferring the Rome Convention into a Regulation (EG-Verordnung) = (Rome I) preserves the rule that the applicable law is the law of the place where the party performing the service characterising the contract has his habitual residence, but it seeks to enhance certainty, *inter alia* by abolishing the exception clause.[191]

The conclusion is that the treaties and the regulation proposal discussed above all use the choice of laws rule that favours the seller's country. It could be argued that such an approach would guarantee uniformity beyond the application of the CISG. The fact is that the rule is simple and easy to administer and avoids the difficulty of changing the applicable law when issues arise, which are not resolved by the CISG.[192] It furthermore avoids the problem of determining issues such as where the contract has been formed or where the contract is being performed, just to mention a few of the considerations to determine the applicable law. As an added advantage, the question of jurisdiction would loose its importance, as in cases of acceptance of the above rule all jurisdiction sought would come up with the same solution, namely the seller's place of business.

The most powerful argument is that most of the European states, as a consequence of the Rome Convention, have accepted the rule that the applicable law is determined by the seller's state. A further argument is that the CISG will not collide with any of the above conventions because the CISG has displaced both the substantive law and the choice of law rules of the *lex causae*.[193]

However, there has been an argument advanced that article 6 of the CISG prevents uniformity in international sales law.[194] Bailey argues that it is impossible to avoid the CISG completely, as suggested by article 6. Article 6 allows a party to derogate or exclude or vary any of the provisions of the CISG. Bailey maintains that article 6 cannot permit parties to avoid CISG rules on contract formation.[195] He continues to argue that article 6 fails to distinguish between two distinct rules in every choice of law analysis, namely:

> (1) the rules applicable to whether the actions of the parties have led to an enforceable (valid) contract and (2) the rules applicable once the contract has been formed.[196]

190 Mather (2001: 184).

191 Art. 4 of the Rome I Proposal reads: '1. To the extent that the law applicable to the contract has not been chosen in accordance with Art. 3, the contract shall be governed by the law determined as follows: (a) a contract of sale shall be governed by the law of the country in which the seller has his habitual residence; (b) [. . .]'.

192 Mather (2001: 186).

193 Bridge (1997: 285).

194 Bailey (1999: 302).

195 Bailey (1999: 302).

196 Bailey (1999: 303).

It is, indeed, strange to suggest that a court must first determine whether there is a valid contract before a choice of law clause can be considered. A contract cannot exist in a legal vacuum, and specifically validity is an issue that can vary between legal systems. Considering article 4, which states that the CISG is not concerned with the validity of a contract, the approach stipulated above leads to a uniform solution, namely via articles 31 or 57, if the requirements of article 1(1)(a) are met. This rule is, of course, subject to article 6. If the parties derogated or are excluded from the CISG and chose another legal system, that system alone is competent to determine whether the contract is valid.

It is singularly unhelpful if a basic principle, as pronounced in article 6, is not understood. The Secretariat Commentary is clear on this matter, as it states that 'parties may exclude [the CISG's] application entirely by choosing a law other than this convention to govern their contract'. [197] It has been wrongly argued that divergence rather than uniformity will result, as a literal interpretation of the Secretariat Commentary suggests that article 6 'is limited to choice of law within a formed contract'.[198] It would be difficult to imagine that a selection of a choice of law is applicable to anything else but a formed contract. If a contract is not formed, then, simply put, the law has no interest in the matter.

This fact makes the matter even worse if the concept of the CISG is not applied and, hence, not understood properly. Bailey argues that:

> Even if the parties later agree that some law other than the CISG governs their contract, it is impossible for them to retroactively undo the negotiations which produced their choice of law clause. The longer the parties wait to exercise their option under Article 6, the greater the proportion of their agreement will be subject to the CISG.[199]

It is difficult to imagine that such a situation is possible because once an express declaration is made which invokes article 6, it will amount at best to a merger clause or simply to a modification of the terms. Hence, all pre-negotiations are now subject to whatever choice of law is made. Pre-negotiations are only of relevance if article 8 or 9 can be invoked. But once the declaration pursuant to article 6 has been made, the CISG is excluded. The proposition that some parts of the contract are subject to the CISG and others are not because suddenly, at one stage, article 6 has been invoked, is untenable. Indeed, great confusion would be created and it would be doubtful if any domestic system would even contemplate following such a proposition. The above argument indicates that the mechanism of article 7 has not been understood and, hence, the 'workings' of the CISG are equally not understood. Article 6, in essence, allows the

197 Commentary on the Draft Convention on Contracts for the International Sale of Goods. Prepared by the Secretariat. Official Records, art 6 cmt. 1.7. U.N. Doc. A/CONF.97/5 (1979{1978 Draft}).
198 Bailey (1999: 304).
199 Bailey (1999: 305).

parties to make a choice, as the CISG is self-inclusive. Once that decision is made, the contract in its totality will be governed by any law other than the CISG. This situation is only changed if a part of the CISG has been excluded. In such a situation, where the parties have not chosen a particular foreign law, a gap has been created which would need to be filled pursuant to article 7(2) of the CISG. If the above argument was to be correct, uniformity would never be achieved and, no doubt, the CISG would already be an instrument academics may talk about, but international trade would already have read the burial rites over the GISG.

The problem in the application of a governing law is primarily when the contract is silent on the matter and not so much if an express choice of law has been made.

IV. The solution to legal diversity under the CISG

As indicated above, articles 31 and 57(1) can be considered to be the default rule, as both articles clearly indicate that they are applicable in a case where there is no specific contractual clause that governs this matter. There is no inconstancy with uniformity if contracts contain express clauses that, as a result, may lead to different solutions. The uniformity in this case rests on the rules within the convention. The CISG has chosen to introduce the general principle of party autonomy pursuant to article 6. This article allows a party to either totally or partially deviate or exclude the CISG. Arguably, the problem is that again only the informed party can make a choice and hence create certainty in their international trade dealings. The problem that cannot be overcome – or at least has not been attempted to be overcome – is that the weaker party is not in a position to object. However, certainty and uniformity have at least been achieved as both parties are aware which law and forum will apply. In other words, despite some underlying problems, a uniform approach has been achieved as article 6[200] allows parties to 'tailor-make' contracts to suit their individual needs.

However, where the inconsistency arises is again in the interpretation of article 6. The fact that a court, pursuant to domestic law, needs to determine issues that are excluded from the CISG and then revert back to the CISG to fill in the remaining issues does not detract from a uniform result. As indicated above, it is the application of a rule that is the deciding factor in determining whether uniformity has been achieved. It is not primarily the outcome that determines uniformity but the correct application of a rule. Conversely, of course, an incorrect application of a rule will detract from the goal of uniformity.

The problem with article 6 is that some commentators and courts believe that an implied exclusion is possible. The drafting history is very clear on this aspect. In ULIS – the forerunner of the CISG – article 3 did provide that a total or

200 Art. states: 'The parties may exclude the application of this Convention or, subject to art. 12, derogate from or vary the effect of any of its provisions.'

partial exclusion of the application of the law 'may be express or implied'.[201] Honnold, one of the drafters of the CISG, notes:

> In UNCITRAL the reference to 'implied' exclusion was deleted on the ground that this language might lead tribunals to exclude the Convention on inadequate grounds: on the other hand, UNCITRAL declined to provide that exclusion must be 'express'.[202]

Courts and tribunals have taken notice of this fact. In a Hamburg Arbitration Proceeding, the arbitrators noted:

> ... Stricter requirements apply to proof of an agreement to exclude the CISG [under its. Art. 6] than those under Art. 3 ... ULIS.[203]

It appears that it is now settled law that a clause stipulating that – as an example – Swiss law will govern a contract is a reference to the CISG.[204] However, earlier in the history of the CISG, such a clause was interpreted as an implicit exclusion of the CISG. As an example, in a Florence Arbitration Proceeding, an express clause in essence indicated that the contract is to be 'governed exclusively by Italian law'.[205] By a majority of two to one, the arbitrators concluded erroneously that this amounted to an implicit exclusion of the CISG.

Despite an extensive jurisprudence, there are still interpreters who do not understand the character of the CISG fully and simply read the Convention article by article. Such a narrow approach is simply not correct and can lead to error. The CISG must be read within its 'four corners' to fully understand the interrelationship of general principles, which occur throughout the Convention.

V. Forum shopping and the CISG

The phenomenon of forum shopping needs to be addressed, as it appears to be a problem which is common to all domestic choice of laws rules. Clearly, the observation can be made that the mere existence of a unified body of law does not prevent forum shopping. The mere possibility of a choice of law implies that forum shopping is not barred. Furthermore, like any international contract, a choice of laws is necessary.

201 Honnold (1999: 78).

202 Honnold (1999: 78).

203 Germany 30 August 1996 Hamburg Arbitration Proceeding [http://cisgw3.law.pace.edu/cases/960830g1.html].

204 There are many rulings on this matter, which are similar. For a good representative sample see Benetton II, OLG Frankfurt, 15 March 1996 [http://cisgw3.law.pace.edu/cases/960315g1.html].

205 Italy 19 April 1994 Florence Arbitration Proceeding [http://cisgw3.law.pace.edu/cases/940419i3.html].

Two arguments can be advanced. First, if a contract is silent, a court in a chosen jurisdiction must determine the applicable law. Courts have two choices: one, they can simply look at their domestic conflict of laws rules and determine the relevant forum which has the closest and real connection to the contract.

As a second option, they may investigate whether a unified law is applicable. In other words, the question is whether the CISG is applicable pursuant to article 1(a). If the answer is 'yes', then articles 31 and 57 will supply the answer and the forum of the seller will supply the relevant domestic law. This is the extent to which the CISG can possibly assist in the selection of the forum.

The only difference with this approach is that the question whether the buyer's and seller's places of business are in a contracting state is asked before a forum has been determined. The only difference is that the questions which must be asked, namely the relevant forum and whether the CISG applies, are asked in a different order. Unless a domestic law makes it mandatory that the forum must be chosen first before the applicable law, this approach cannot be dismissed without cause. After all, once a forum has been chosen and the particular forum is a contracting state the CISG becomes applicable. The advantage of such an approach is that forum shopping is eliminated. However, at the same time the possibility of choosing the most appropriate forum for the claimant has also been curtailed. The question, however, still remains whether all courts would approach this problem in the same way. The answer is clearly no. Assuming that a plaintiff chooses a jurisdiction which is not in a contracting state, the matter, that is, the selection of the forum, takes a different turn. The possibility arises that the CISG could be excluded completely, despite the fact that buyer and seller have their business in a contracting state.

Such an approach would contribute towards uniformity. Contracting parties simply know that the seller's place of business is the relevant forum, and hence, the applicable domestic law is predetermined.

However, if the CISG were applied via article 1(1)(b), a domestic choice of laws determination would need to point to a relevant forum where the CISG is applicable. The argument that this does not promote uniformity must be addressed. It has been argued that the CISG creates a distinction between two types of international contracts, namely those where the CISG applies and others which are subject to domestic laws. Such a view is quite correct and can be enlarged with the observation that not all states have adopted the CISG. It is a logical conclusion that in cases where the CISG does not apply, forum shopping can provide significant advantages to one party.

However, a better argument is that the CISG has widened its influence through article 1(1)(b). The CISG is not only applicable where both parties have their business in contracting states but also where a domestic choice of laws clause points to a forum in a contracting state. The only difference between article (1(1)(a)) and 1(1)(b) is the method by which the applicable law is determined. A different method needs to be applied which, in essence, is outside the general principles of the CISG and must be filled pursuant to article 7(2) by domestic law.

In other words, the advocated approach is still in line with the mandate of article 7 and, hence, contributes towards uniformity.

The same can be said if a party takes advantage of the principle of party autonomy and selects a particular forum, which best suits the needs of the party and is most beneficial for the party concerned. Ferrari is correct in pointing out that 'an international uniform contract law convention cannot prevent forum shopping…it can [only] reduce the possibility'.[206]

C. Conclusion

This chapter has suggested that the CISG supplies a default rule in articles 31 and 57, which allows parties to reduce their costs of contracting. A uniform law will reduce the costs of contracting, as there is no need to bargain around initial allocations. This concept has found its intellectual heritage in the Coarse theorem that suggests that the law should be structured in a way that it reduces the costs of contracting.[207] The CISG has been structured in such a way, as a uniform law promotes certainty, and furthermore, it should appeal to parties as an alternative formulation. It could be argued that the default rule in the CISG due to its 'international flavor' would be the one parties would select with full information and costless contracting and hence become an 'untailored default rule'.[208]

The advantage of such a rule would be that it would overcome the problem of courts misconstruing interpretations of conflict of laws if the parties opted out of a standard default rule. This is so because not only the substantive law but also the choice of laws rule are contained in the same uniform rules and hence an interpretation would rely on the same principle, namely article 7.

Central to the suggestion that the CISG provides a choice of laws rule is that courts have the ability to give a uniform effect to contracts where the parties have not made an express choice as to the applicable forum and hence applicable law. The CISG does not completely overcome the problem of forum shopping, but it reduces it significantly. The second point is that the CISG will overcome anomalies produced by varied domestic private international law rules, as a uniform default rule is created. The third point is that courts do make mistakes and the CISG offers a uniform and simplified approach to the choice of the governing law, which, no doubt, will enhance predictability and reduce the costs of contracting. Nothing explains this fact better than arbitral decisions. Many arbitration rules require arbitrators to take account of trade usage and provisions of the contract. Simply put, arbitral procedural rules allow arbitrators to choose the applicable substantive law in cases where parties have not made a relevant express determination. As seen in an ICC decision,[209] the CISG was

206 Ferrari (2002a: 689).
207 See Whincop and Keyes (1997: 523).
208 Whincop and Keyes (1997: 525).
209 ICC Court of Arbitration No 5713/1989, Yearbook of Commercial Arbitration (1990), 70.

chosen despite the fact that neither of the parties had their place of business in a contracting state.

> there is no better source to determine the prevailing trade usages than the terms of the UN Convention on the International Sale of Goods. [210]

Arguably, a choice of laws decision has been made but the crucial point is that the CISG was viewed as the 'best fitting' solution to a trade dispute. In sum, the CISG has the ability to view 'the proper law of the contract as a supplement to contractual bargaining [and is therefore] the first step in making [choice of laws] more transparent, more efficient and more pragmatic'.[211]

210 ICC Court of Arbitration No 5713/1989, Yearbook of Commercial Arbitration (1990), 70.
211 Whincop and Keyes (1997: 543).

Chapter 6

Specific performance and article 28 CISG

A. Specific performance and the rules of the forum

Article 28 is one of the examples in the CISG that demonstrates the compromise that was necessary to reconcile common law and civil law traditions in the uniform international legal regime.[212] It reads as follows:

> If, in accordance with the provisions of this Convention, one party is entitled to require performance of any obligations by the other party, a court is not bound to enter a judgment for specific performance unless the court would do so under its own law in respect of similar contracts of sale not governed by this Convention.

A theoretical construction and logical extension of article 28 would lead to the conclusion that this article is divisive and does not contribute towards a uniform application of the CISG. From this point of view, it would be correct to argue that the judicial willingness to order specific performance 'may vary dramatically in accordance with the *lex fori*'.[213] Such an outcome would greatly diminish the effectiveness of the CISG, as the remedial system plays an important role. Farnsworth noted:

> No aspect of a system of contract law is more revealing of its underlying assumption than is the law that prescribes the relief available for breach.[214]

However, article 28 also demonstrates that a potentially divisive rule was in practice ignored and a uniform approach was taken. As it will be shown below, a strict adherence to the letter of the law was replaced by a pragmatic approach. This can be demonstrated by the fact that there is only one recorded decision in

212 Gabriel (2004: 99).
213 Herman (2003: 5).
214 Farnsworth (1979: 676).

which the court dealt with article 28 in length, namely *Magellan International Co v Salzgitter Handel GmbH,*[215] and that decision was a pragmatic one.

Before analysing the effect of article 28 and the possible consequences on uniformity, a clear understanding of specific performance must be demonstrated. Specific performance is a remedy for a breach of a contract which is not satisfied by granting damages. The position of the common law is that it only allows specific performance in cases where damages would be inadequate.[216]

B. Domestic rules of specific performance

The problem of article 28 began at the Drafting Conference, where a sharp division among the delegates based on their domestic origins ended up in a compromise. Again, it highlights the difficulties where the question of 'domestic law' needs to be addressed. Admittedly, there is no confusion if article 28 is applied by the forum and, hence, a court applies its own domestic law which it is familiar with. However, if foreign law needs to be applied, a potential problem can arise, which would not only result in wrong decisions, but would undermine uniformity. If 'Civilian' or 'Common Law' or 'Anglo-American' terminology is used, an oversimplification of the problem of applying the correct law has started.

The expression 'under its own law' in article 28 is a precise term and cannot be filled by either of these groupings. As an example, the Anglo-American orbit contains differences that are far reaching and would lead to different results. In the United Kingdom, differences exist between English and Scottish Law. Furthermore, it is highly speculative at this stage how article 28 would be applied in the United Kingdom as the latter only participated in the drafting stage, but never felt it necessary to become a signatory to the CISG despite the fact that the CISG is the *de facto* sales law in the EU. In the American part of the equation, the same differences can be observed. To speak of 'United States commercial law is a misnomer, as it is a patchwork sewn together state by state.'[217] As an example, in Louisiana, Civil Law still has its applications.

The same can be said in relation to the Civil System of law. For example, although Germany, France and Switzerland commit to specific performance, Spain, despite being in the same 'camp', seems to be more dedicated to awarding this type of relief than the other three countries. Italy, on the other hand, prefers damages to specific performance.[218]

For the purpose of this analysis, only some countries will be examined. It will be sufficient to draw some conclusions. It has been argued that the United States would deny performance requests in all but the most exceptional circumstances.[219]

215 [http://cisgw3.law.pace.edu/cases/991207u1.html].

216 See *Cud v Rutter* (1720) 24 ER 521.

217 Herman (2003: 9).

218 Herman (2003: 10).

219 Herman (2003: 208).

However, this assumption was based on the old article 2 of the UCC. The revised article 2-716 and 2-709 do provide for 'specific performance by the buyer as well as a concomitant action for the price by the seller in appropriate circumstances'.[220] According to Gabriel,

> given the recent changes in the American domestic sales law which provides for the parties to agree upon specific performance as a remedy; it is unlikely that there will be any significant development of case law in the United States denying specific performance under the Convention.[221]

It would be doubtful, having regard to UCC 2-716 and 2-709, that a court would not allow specific performance, especially when considering that the UCC allows for specific performance when the claimant is unable to execute a cover purchase.[222]

C. The CISG and specific performance

The CISG departs from the Common Law rule and includes specific performance into its remedy regime. It constitutes one of the remedies open to the aggrieved party, along with, *inter alia*, an avoidance of the contract or a reduction of the price, or damages, which can be claimed instead of or additionally to the aforementioned remedies.[223]

Specific performance is mentioned in several articles. According to article 30, the buyer has the right to demand delivery of the goods or the documents representing the goods; under article 46, the buyer can demand performance by the seller of 'his obligations'. The seller can demand payment of the price pursuant to article 62 or demand that the buyer take delivery under article 60. Honnold specifically points out that the scope of the remedy to require specific performance was 'one of the most stubborn issues encountered in the preparation of the uniform rules'.[224] The important point to note is that Honnold, one of the drafters of the CISG, was aware that the purpose of the Convention was to provide uniform rules. As such, every attempt, as difficult as it may have been, was made to achieve the stated goal of uniformity.

220 Gabriel (2004: 102).

221 Gabriel (2004: 100).

222 Gabriel (2004: 99 fn 435).

223 Art. 45 (buyer's remedies) and art. 61 (seller's remedies), which set out the general range of remedies, state that either buyer or seller are not deprived of any right 'he may have to claim damages by exercising his right to other remedies'. It follows, therefore, that any remedy which is incorporated into art. 45 always leaves the door open to claim damages in addition to any other remedy such as specific performance.

224 Honnold (1999: 218).

A further point needs to be noted, namely that the buyer's[225] right to demand specific performance is not unlimited. Article 77 requires the parties to mitigate any loss. Looking at article 28, an application of article 77 poses some problems. If the *lex fori* of a country awards specific performance as a primary remedy, a plaintiff might try to sidestep mitigation altogether by insisting on performance.[226] If such an approach were taken, the question would arise whether the principle of good faith can be relied upon.

Two arguments would follow from such a consideration. The first argument would suggest that there is no principle such as good faith among the parties, because article 7(1), which mentions 'good faith', refers to the interpretation of the Convention only.[227]According to the second argument, article 7(1) is not applicable to the described situation, since a remedy is sought which is consistent with the particular domestic law and, hence, the CISG is not applicable. Or, thirdly, it can be argued that a duty to mitigate applies in any case, irrespective of whether article 28 is invoked or not. Arguably therefore, the potential for a non-uniform application of the CISG is a real problem. However, it could be said that article 77 refers to a duty to mitigate the loss and, hence, a duty to mitigate applies in all circumstances. The matter, though, remains unclear, as the party requiring specific performance might abandon the right to damages. In this case article 77 will not be applicable.

However, the CISG has somewhat narrowed the field in the possibility of requiring performance, as in most articles, a restriction or exemption is also embedded. Article 46 can be used as an example to illustrate the point. Article 46(1) requires the court or tribunal to only allow specific performance where the buyer has not resorted to a remedy which is 'inconsistent with this requirement'. Furthermore, in article 46(2), specific performance is restricted to cases where the non-conformity of the delivered goods amounts to fundamental breach. Pursuant to article 46(3), the seller may be required to repair the goods unless it is unreasonable for him to do so. Furthermore, article 86(1) requires that the buyer take all reasonable steps to preserve the goods if he intends to reject them, and article 88(2) notes that perishable goods need to be resold. These provisions limit the buyer's right to specific performance to situations where he has a practical interest in specific performance indeed.

Above all, the CISG limits specific performances pursuant to article 7(1), which requires an application of the principle of good faith. Specific performance where the price has dramatically changed in the market place

225 As the rights of seller and buyer are tracking each other, only the buyer's rights are discussed, unless a right is specifically addressing the seller.

226 Herman (2003: 8).

227 A dispute can be found in the literature whether art. 7(1) refers to 'good faith' between the parties or to 'good faith' in the interpretation of the Convention only. The views are divided. For further analysis see Schlechtriem (2005); Felemegas (2003). Felemegas argues that it only refers to the interpretation of the Convention. For the opposing view see Zeller (2003).

would be difficult to enforce, as it would be in breach of good faith. It could be argued that 'coerced performances' would fall under the same category, namely a breach of good faith.

D. Article 28 and procedural law

A reading of article 28 does not make it clear whether the court whose law would not provide for the remedy of specific performance in the particular situation is obliged to deny specific performance, as article 28 speaks of the court's 'not [being] bound to enter a judgment for specific performance'. It might be argued that a court may choose to enforce article 28 and not grant any specific performance. However, Honnold suggests that it means that a court, 'if it would not require performance under its own law[,] is free to either require performance or to apply other remedies'.[228] It appears that reading the article in a holistic fashion, weight must be given to the word 'unless', which suggests that Honnold's view should prevail.

Another problem which article 28 creates is the notion of 'own law in respect of similar contracts of sale not governed by this convention'. Two points of view are defendable. Article 28 might either call for the law of the forum, or it might imply that the law of private international law will determine the governing law, which then is applied to the circumstances. In the only decided case[229] on this matter, the court did not look at the domestic conflict of laws rule but looked at its own law, which is 'consistent with what commentators have long speculated the proper result should be'.[230]

Furthermore, the CISG in many of the articles dealing with specific performance notes that the 'buyer may require performance', as in article 46(1). However, the CISG does not explain what measures a court should employ to enforce performance, nor what measure a court should employ to 'require' the performance of the contract.[231]

The problem is that these matters are procedural in nature and would need to be solved by the law of the forum. Honnold states that the framers of specifically article 28 worked from the assumption that procedural rules are different in Common Law and Civil Law countries and, hence, due to deference to the relevant fora, the procedural aspects were left out of the Convention. However, subsequent comparative studies have found that the difference is not as great as had been supposed,[232] and they might become even smaller facing recent developments in the unification of procedural law. Only recently has a joint study group of the American Law Institute and UNIDROIT (the ALI/UNIDROIT study group)

228 Honnold (1988: 224).
229 See fn 215 above.
230 Gabriel (2004: 100).
231 Honnold (1988: 219).
232 Honnold (1988: 219).

put a determinable starting point to this unification process by publishing the Principles and Rules of Transnational Civil Procedure in 2004.[233] The study group attempted to overcome the tensions not only between the civil and common procedural law but also those that were unique to the United States and others and 'succeeded admirably in easing the tensions and in taking advantage of unprecedented open-mindedness on the part of legislatures and practitioners'.[234]

With regard to article 28, the fact is that the measures a court may employ to enforce performance leave a gap, which needs to be filled by domestic law pursuant to article 7(2). It should be stressed that it is not due to the fact that the rules requiring performance are procedural in nature that a domestic solution is required. The CISG comprises many articles that, in several systems, are procedural in nature. Awarding damages under article 74 for attorney's fees is such an example. The simple fact is that gap filling according to article 7(2) is relevant whenever a gap exists; whether the gap is procedural or substantive in nature does not matter.

E. Article 28 and the conflict of laws rules

I. Specific performance regularly granted under the CISG

Article 28 invites domestic rules to prevail over the rules of the Convention. It must be mentioned again that so far only one case, which took particular note of article 28, has been reported. All the speculation that article 28 would lead to forum shopping and hence undermine the uniform sales law has not proven to be right. Kastely argued that:

> Article 28 makes the availability of specific performance dependent on the law of the forum, parties will be encouraged to forum-shop for a national court system that will or will not grant specific performance.[235]

II. Article 28 as a mere option

It would not be exaggerated to say that many cases have been decided granting specific performance to buyers or sellers. The reason why the courts did not invoke article 28 is twofold. First, article 28 is declaratory in nature and gives courts and tribunals the option of whether they wish to invoke a domestic rule. The point that a 'court is not bound to enter a judgment for specific performance' does not say that it cannot enter judgment. Article 28 allows courts and tribunals to use their discretionary powers. Courts and tribunals have simply ignored the option given by article 28 and opted to apply the uniform rule instead.

233 See Uniform Law Review (2004).
234 Nhlapo (2004: 811).
235 Kastely (1988: 615).

In *Magellan International v Salzgitter Handel*,[236] the court argued 'that article 46(1) would appear to make specific performance routinely available under the Convention. But article 28 conditions the availability of specific performance'.[237] The court then investigated the relevant provision of the UCC and came to the conclusion that Magellan proved the fact that specific performance should be granted. Of special significance to the court was that the purchaser could not cover reasonably with a substitute action and Magellan had already paid the price for the goods. This appears to be consistent with § 2-716 of the UCC.

III. Article 28 designed for common law courts

The second reason why article 28 has not prevented any claims for specific performance hitherto is a practical one: the courts concerned with a claim for performance resided in civil law countries. As pointed out in the beginning, specific performance is the primary remedy in civil law systems, which is why article 28 is not affected. This is particularly made clear by the judgment of the District Court Schaffhausen where the court laconically noted that 'the right to specific performance is always given'.[238]

There is a multitude of cases where specific performance was not granted but where article 28 was not relied upon.[239] The argument can be advanced that courts took note of article 28 and simply assumed that domestic law is not in variance with the CISG.

As far as article 62 is concerned, it has been applied 93 times. The same finding as with article 46 applies here as well, namely that article 28 has never been mentioned in all cases dealing with the seller's right to demand the price. The Commercial Court of St Gallen noted what should be obvious and perhaps lies at the heart of the problem in relation to article 28, namely that 'all buyers must know that, as far as the opposing party did not default in performing the contract, they are obliged to pay the purchase price agreed upon'.[240] In that sense,

236 United States, 7 December 1999 Federal Dist C [Illinois] [http://cisgw3.law.pace.edu/cases/991207u1.html] (previously cited differently, see. n. 215).

237 United States, 7 December 1999 Federal Dist Ct [Illinois] [http://cisgw3.law.pace.edu/cases/991207u1.html].

238 Switzerland, 25 February 2002, [http://cisgw3.law.pace.edu/cases/020225s1.html].

239 Appellate Court of Hamm, Germany, 9 June 1995, 11 U 191/94.[http://cisgw3.law.pace.edu/cases/950609g1.html]; Austrian Supreme Court, Oberster Gerichtshof, 14 January 2002, 7 Ob 301/01t, citing the decision by the Oberlandesgericht Linz (GZ 11 R 167/01k-67) [http://cisgw3.law.pace.edu/cases/020114a.3.html].

240 Switzerland, 29 April 2004, 20040429 [http://cisgw3.law.pace.edu/cases/040429s1.html]. Many other courts follow the Swiss ruling by stating that 'based on [art. 62] the seller has the right to demand that the buyer pay the price'. See *Jose Luis Morales v Nez Marketing*, Mexico 4 May 1993, Compromex Arbitration proceeding M/66/92 [http://cisgw3.law.pace.edu/cases/930504m1.html]; several Russian Arbitration proceedings unhesitantly noted that it is 'an obligation of the buyer under articles 53 and 62 CISG to pay off his debt for the goods received'. See Russia, 6 October 1998, 269/1997 [http://cisgw3.law.pace.edu/cases/981006r1.html] also see [http://cisgw3.law.pace.edu/cases/970611r1.html]; Russian Arbitration, [http://cisgw3.law.pace.edu/cases/97012r1.html].

a specific performance to pay the price is merely what is right and just, and it would be difficult to see that any other remedy would be appropriate to put the seller into the very position he would have been in had the contract been properly performed. The mandate that the aggrieved party is to be put in the position it would have been in if the contract had been performed properly is contained in article 74. It is not surprising that courts and tribunals see neither the value nor the need to resort to domestic law when the CISG is perfectly clear in allowing a remedy that is appropriate and, furthermore, would be difficult to change. If a buyer does not pay the price, what else is there to be done but demand payment? The fact that it is termed a 'specific performance' is merely coincidental and a court would be hard pressed to find another remedy which is defendable and just. It can be argued that specific performances, which are contained in the CISG, are so obvious and clear that there is really no viable alternative but to grant these remedies. This is especially so, as the CISG also included 'stoppers' that need to be overcome before specific performance can be claimed.

F. Conclusion

Article 28 shows that, sometimes, a political compromise is plainly ignored, as after the 'heat of the battle' those entrusted with the application of the law will ask, 'what was that all about?'

At the Drafting Conference, those arguing that performance is the primary remedy for breach and those arguing that the primary remedy is damages were on a collision course. This was averted by the compromise which is now article 28. Schlechtriem noted:

> Right from the beginning of discussions on Uniform Sales Law, there seemed no prospect of bridging the different approaches adopted by the different legal systems. Rabel had said that the conflicting basic approaches could not be eradicated or fused. The problem was therefore solved by means of compromise: a court is to treat an action for specific performance as it would under its own law (*lex fori*). Courts of contracting states which grant specific performance only as an exceptional remedy are not required to alter fundamental principles of their judicial procedure. It is a matter of judicial procedure and substantive law.[241]

Interestingly, jurisprudence from all 'camps' does not suggest that there is a collision course. Arguably, despite earlier misgivings, specific performance has not taken on the mantle of a primary remedy but has merged into the total regime of remedial measures, as it is merely one small part of the total scheme.

241 Schlechtriem and Schwenzer (2005: 200).

It would make no sense if a party required completion of a contract if it could merely ask for damages. Honnold, in an example, points to a buyer who lost the on-selling contract and has no need for the goods anymore but the seller insists on completing the contract. Arguably, such a demand for specific performance would not pass the general principle of mitigating damages, as extra costs, such as shipping costs, would eventuate.

There are too many restrictions, such as the duty to mitigate losses, which in effect diminish the possible primary position of a specific performance. Arguably, courts and tribunals look at the total remedial scheme and narrow the choice down to the most appropriate one in the circumstances, giving effect not only to the relevant articles, but also to articles 8 and 7. The four-corner rule is tacitly applied and, hence, recourse to article 28 will often not be necessary. Uniformity of application, applying pragmatic standards, has overcome what might be called a political or scholarly hurdle.

Chapter 7

Gap filling and unification

Where are the boundaries?

A. Gaps and exclusions

As seen in Chapter 4, the CISG is not a complete statement of law and hence gaps exist, which need to be filled by domestic law. Because external gaps are inevitable, the choice of law question can never be eliminated. Such a choice of law has no effect on the application of the unified parts of contract law within the CISG. The choice of law will determine which municipal system of law must be used to fill external gaps.

Unification of law can only be achieved step by step.[242] In this chapter, it is not envisaged to explain how gaps are to be filled, but rather what effect gaps have on the uniform application of an international sales convention. For the purpose of this book, this chapter will only take a close look at article 4 and by necessity, when required, article 7. It will serve as an example where gap filling can advance the uniform character of the CISG and demonstrate that gaps are not necessarily a detractor to the goal of uniformity.

Of central concern to the question of a uniform approach to conventions is that uniformity is not only a question of matters that are included in the convention but also a question of what has been excluded. A uniform approach has to extend to the inclusive as well as exclusive rules. Only when this 'dual approach' is taken can a politically acceptable and economically useful result be obtained. The CISG left a space free, which must be covered either by domestic law or possibly by other conventions.[243]

The first point to consider is that the CISG makes a clear distinction between gaps and exclusions. Article 7(2) provides the method that needs to be adopted in cases where there is a gap or exclusion of a matter within the CISG. In other words, the 'depth of regulation'[244] is set by article 7(2), which states:

> (2) Questions concerning matters governed by this Convention which are not expressly settled in it are to be settled in conformity with the general principles

242 Enderlein and Maskow (1992: 39).
243 Enderlein and Maskow (1992: 39).
244 Enderlein and Maskow (1992: 39).

> on which it is based or, in the absence of such principles, in conformity with the law applicable by virtue of the rules of private international law.

If an issue is not excluded by the convention, the conflict of laws rule does not need to be applied. However, if there are either no general principles within the CISG or the matter is explicitly excluded, a domestic law needs to be consulted to resolve the issue, hence invoking conflict of laws issues.

The general principle of validity of contract is such an example. Drobnig justifies its exclusion by stating that:

> [t]he difficulties in this area are due in part to the legal complexities and to divergent social policies, in part also to conceptual complications.[245]

Article 4 has been described as a 'contractual scheme [of] uncertain functional characteristics'.[246] It is not surprising to see different views emerging in relation to the interpretation and also to the function of article 4.

Hartnell suggests that the validity question poses a danger to the development of a coherent jurisprudence of international trade by giving courts and tribunals wide discretion to determine when to apply domestic law.[247] Such a view is far too narrow and ignores the application of article 7, which sets the boundaries between provisions within the CISG.

B. Concurrent contract and product liability claims

An example of a specific exclusion is article 5 which states that:

> This Convention does not apply to the liability of the seller for death or personal injury caused by the goods to any person.

Article 5 alludes to product liability, which in some cases is a matter in tort. In this case, the conflict of laws issue is clear, namely that such matters are excluded from the CISG, as the convention only applies to contractual matters.

This is exactly the point where disagreements in the interpretation of article 5 may eventuate and the 'CISG will invariably come into conflict with extant choice of law issues'.[248] It appears settled that if a buyer claims personal injury from the seller, article 5 would disallow such a claim to be governed by the CISG.

Article 5 by necessity needs to be read in conjunction with article 2, which specifically excludes sales for personal, family, or household use, and article 1(1), which speaks of 'places of *business*'. As such, it ought to be clear that the CISG

245 Drobnig (1986: 313).
246 Ferrari (1995: 4).
247 Hartnell (1993: 3).
248 Pribetic (2004).

only applies to claims emanating from business transactions. Schlechtriem also noted in his Commentary on Oberlandesgericht Düsseldorf 2 July 1993, 'domestic rules on product liability are not supposed to be "disturbed" by the Convention'.[249]

However, the situation can be different when the buyer is being sued by a third party for liability and then wishes to be reimbursed by the original seller. The question then is whether this is a third party claim or whether this matter is an issue that emanates directly from the contractual relationship between buyer and seller. Schlechtriem's view is that:

> [i]f the buyer were allowed to claim his sub-purchaser's injuries as damages of his own, product liability would indeed collide with sales law remedies under the Convention[250]

The UNCITRAL Digest of case law[251] argues in a similar fashion and points out the following:

> Since liability for death or personal injury 'to any person' is excluded from the Convention's scope of application, it was suggested that the buyer's claims for pecuniary loss resulting from a claim against the buyer for personal injury caused by the goods should be outside the Convention as well.[252]

The problem with the above reasoning is that it does not take account of article 7(2), which urges interpreters to take note of general principles. Pecuniary losses of any kind should be treated equally under the principle of full compensation pursuant to article 74. Only with the general principle of full compensation in mind can uniformity be achieved.

The problem which needs to be addressed is the fact that a monetary loss has occurred and that article 74 is very particular in addressing this issue. Article 74 allows a party to claim damages caused by a breach of the contract. The aim is to place a party in a position where it would have been if the contract had been performed properly. These losses can take the form of direct losses, incidental losses, or other losses consequential upon the breach.[253] Therefore, arguably, article 5 does not apply, as otherwise domestic and foreign litigants will face the prospect of uncertainty and increased transactional costs.[254]

One of the problems affecting a monetary claim based on a previous potential tortious action is the question as to the phrasing of the claim. If a pecuniary loss due to injury would be claimed, the situation is that an action in torts is no

249 Schlechtriem, see [http://cisgw3.law.pace.edu/cases/930702g1.html#add].
250 Schlechtriem, see [http://cisgw3.law.pace.edu/cases/930702g1.html#add].
251 See [http://cisgw3.law.pace.edu/cisg/text/anno-art-05.html#udftn2].
252 See [http://cisgw3.law.pace.edu/cisg/text/anno-art-05.html#udftn2].
253 Zeller (2005: 120).
254 Pribetic (2004).

longer of relevance. Hence all matters of economic loss, except the one caused by injury to a third party, can be claimed under the CISG. It is logically difficult to distinguish one kind of reimbursement from the other one just because the original loss had its foundation in tort. Admittedly, this would not be a situation that could develop very often. Article 5 has only been used twice in 20 years and both cases date back 10 years.[255]

The next point to consider has been alluded to by Schlechtriem when he noted that there is a possible overlap between domestic tort actions and matters settled within the CISG. He notes:

> If a domestic tort law protects the expectations of a buyer with regards to the quality of goods and thereby concurs with matters genuinely governed by CISG, it is sufficient to adjust the 'concurring' tort action to the rules of CISG.[256]

Arguably, the question of recouping losses due to injury caused by defective goods is also governed by the CISG. It is clear that article 74 can be used with the obvious proviso that matters such as proper notification pursuant to article 38 are adhered to and the damage must have been reasonably foreseeable.

The burden of foreseeability is not a difficult one, as the plaintiff in the original case already needs to establish that the defendant owed a duty of care, that the duty has been breached and that the damages flowed directly from such a breach.[257] The problem is whether article 74 allows consequential damages to be part of its regime. Arguably, that is the case, as all damages that are consequences of a breach of a contract are allowable. Under the CISG, a consequential action, which is based on a tort action, can be covered under article 35. There is no debate that if a buyer sells the goods and they prove to be unsuitable he then can claim remedies from the original seller under article 45. If that is the case, there is no difference between a claim based solely on the unsuitability of the goods and a claim based on inquiry caused to a person. Why should such a claim be disallowed just because the injured person mounted an action in tort?

The simple fact is that the injury only occurred because the goods did not conform to article 35. Hence, monetary third party claims should not logically be excluded. Admittedly, because of article 5, a claim between a buyer and seller that is based on tort law must be excluded from the CISG. However, the definition of consequential damages should be enlarged to allow third party claims based on defective goods that have caused damages to a third party to be included. Simply put:

> If Article 5 of the CISG contemplates product liability property damage claims, then the objective of 'decisional harmony' between inter-provincial

255 See [http://cisgw3.law.pace.edu/cisg/text/anno-art-05.html].
256 Schlechtriem (1988: 472).
257 See *Donoghue v Stevenson* [1932] AC 562.

> and international cases, and the goals of certainty, predictability and international comity, all favour the *lex loci* contractus over the *lex fori* for choice-of-law under the rubric of the CISG.[258]

Arguably, if the above proves to be the correct way to go, there is no obstacle to include also product liability cases, which are founded in tort but are consequential in nature, that is, a 'middleman' is the plaintiff.

It is argued that, as the focus of the CISG is to unify international sales laws, article 5 must be read within the context and focus of the CISG. It must be interpreted expansively and not narrowly. It is clear and settled law that a seller is not liable for personal injury under the CISG but under tort law. In that case, the *locus delicti*, that is the place of injury, will supply the relevant law. In respect of concurrent contractual and tortious liability claim, the suggestion is made that the 'place of injury' is less relevant than the *situs* of the contract, 'based on the view that without privity in contract, the concurrent tort would not arise. Simply put the *lex foci conventionis* is the new frame of reference'.[259] It is important to remember what Kötz wrote in response to achieving the goal of uniformity.

> The question appears justified whether uniform law, in as far as it intends to simplify laws, does not find itself in the position of Heracles who cut off Hydra's snake head only to be confronted with three new ones instead.[260]

As explained above, if a narrow and over-technical view is taken, a fragmentation of what starts out as a simple exercise can overshadow the stated goal of uniformity. This is especially so as with this solution an otherwise untidy problem of *depeçage* can be avoided. It is argued that only if it is absolutely impossible to find recourse within the CISG should an interpreter turn to domestic law in order to avoid the creation of 'Hydra's three heads', specifically when interpreting article 4.

C. Article 4(a): validity exclusion

Generally speaking, article 4 excludes from the CISG matters of validity and third party claims. This article reflects the compromise between the political ambitions of sovereign states and the need for international commerce. This compromise enables contracting states to enforce traditional limitations on party autonomy.[261] The problem courts and tribunals are faced with is to distinguish

258 Pribetic (2004).
259 Pribetic (2004).
260 Kötz (1986: 7).
261 Hartnell (1993: 7).

between issues governed by the CISG and issues of validity which are excluded. Hartnell succinctly observed that:

> this fundamental tension is often left to slumber through scholarly discussions of the proper interpretation of the validity exclusion, like a dog that, it is feared, would disturb the peace if roused.[262]

The drafting history of the CISG suggests that the validity issue was intended to be a loophole which could serve municipal ambitions in relation to domestic policies. It is therefore not surprising that article 4 is ambiguous and can mean different things to different people.[263]

Not surprisingly, two problematic issues can be readily discovered in article 4(a) that states that 'except as otherwise expressly provided in this Convention' the CISG 'is not concerned with (a) the validity of the contract or any of its provisions or of any usage'.

The first problem is that the CISG does not exclude validity *per se*, as the convention is concerned with some validity issues. Hartnell correctly pointed out that:

> tribunals should not allow the language of 'mandatory law' to seduce them into thinking that the task of interpreting article 4(a) is nothing more than a conflict of laws problem. Determining which validity issues are preserved to domestic law requires a careful balancing between the international character of the Convention and the public policies which forced the political compromise embodied in article 4(a).[264]

The mandate is clear. The defining point is that these issues must be expressly stated within the four corners of the CISG. Literally taken, if validity is not stated within a provision in an express fashion, it is excluded pursuant to article 4. However, this argument does not hold. Article 7 specifically explains the interpretation ladder which includes general principles as being part of the CISG.

Arguably, all those issues, which are governed by general principles as provided for in article 7(2),[265] can be considered as being expressly stated within the Convention. This is in line with the mandate of uniformity. However, on certain matters, complete agreement and hence uniformity has not been initially achieved. An example is the question of the burden of proof. At the beginning,

262 Hartnell (1993: 2).

263 See Commentary on the [1978] Draft Convention on Contracts for the International Sale of Goods, Prepared by the Secretariat. U.N. Doc A/CONF 97/5 (1979).

264 Hartnell (1993: 93).

265 Art. 7(2) states: 'Questions concerning matters governed by this Convention which are not expressly settled in it are to be settled in conformity with the general principles on which it is based or, in the absence of such principles, in conformity with the law applicable by virtue of the rules of private international law'.

the issue was felt to fall outside the CISG due to article 4. The Bezirksgericht der Saane ruled that the burden of proof falls within article 4 and hence the matter must be resolved by domestic law.[266] Another Swiss decision found that questions regarding the burden of proof are not governed by the CISG but that due to 'the underlying systematic structure certain principles may be inferred'.[267]

The uncertainty with regard to the burden of proof indicates that the CISG must be read within its four corners. Such a reading will supply an answer, as no article on its own will be able to solve all possible situations. It follows that 'the party who invokes a right bears the burden of proof to its establishment of that right and, on the other hand, the other party must prove any facts that exclude the invoked claim'.[268] The conclusion is that the burden of proof can shift within the dictates of a single article.[269]

The second point is that the CISG does not make it clear which are 'validity' issues. To solve the problem posed by article 4, a two-tiered approach is necessary. First, a court would need to ask itself whether the CISG governs the issue at hand. If so, the matter is resolved and no recourse to a domestic law is necessary. As an example, if the question would arise whether a contract has been validly concluded the answer lies within the CISG because the convention explicitly deals with the formation of contracts.[270] Article 4 therefore would not be applicable.

If the answer is no, the question would need to be asked whether the issue at hand is in reality one of validity. A good example is the common law question of consideration. An offer is considered to be not binding if consideration is lacking. However, under the mandate of the CISG, consideration is not required. The CISG lists the matters that are required for a contract to be valid and hence expressly removes the principle of consideration from article 4(a). However, such an approach is not without its critics. The main argument is that if this approach would be taken, a validity issue would never arise and therefore the 'expressly provided exception' in article 4 would be redundant.[271] The problem with this approach is that not all matters, which, as an example, fall under 'mistake' can be accommodated within the CISG. Once a matter falls outside the CISG, domestic law needs to be applied, and before that can happen, a particular label must be given to the problem in order to find the appropriate domestic law.

Once a gap is discovered which cannot be filled by the CISG, a domestic law would need to be applied. A domestic law can only be applied once the issue has been properly identified, that is, a label has been given. Hence, matters of

266 Switzerland 20 February 1997, [http://cisgw3.law.pace.edu/cases/97022s1.html].

267 Switzerland 30 November 1998 Handelsgericht Zürich [http://cisgw3.law.pace.edu/cases/981130s1.html].

268 Bundesgerichtshof, Germany, 9 January 2002, [http:// cisgw3.law.pace.edu/cases/020109g1.html].

269 DiMatteo, Dhooge, Greene, Maurer, and Pagnattaro (2004: 436).

270 ICC Arbitration Case No 7399 of 1993 [http://cisgw3.law.pace.edu/cases/937399i1.html].

271 Lessiak (1989: 492).

validity not governed by the CISG would need to be resolved by validity laws of the relevant domestic law. Article 4 specifically is an elastic exception and should therefore accommodate changes in international commercial practices, which of course would 'further the goals of uniformity and predictability'.[272]

In sum, the first step is to see whether the CISG supplies an answer. Only if all avenues are exhausted should recourse to domestic law be sought. Article 7(2) clearly describes the mechanism by which the process will be affected. With such an approach, courts are not tempted to 'fall back' onto domestic rules and, hence, approach the CISG in an ethnocentric fashion. As an example, the problem of interpreting disclaimers of implied warranties can be used. In the United States, § 2-316 of the UCC are validity rules, which, as terms, become ineffective unless certain words or types of words are used.[273] Furthermore, sections 2-316 and 2-302 are concerned with preventing unfair surprises, and especially § 2-302's unconscionability rule concerns validity.[274]

A court looking at article 4 and noting that disclaimers are validity issues pursuant to the UCC could come erroneously to the conclusion that pursuant to article 4, domestic rules need to be applied. However, the CISG deals with matters of disclaimers not in an express fashion but by recourse to general principles. First, the principles of good faith pursuant to article 7(1) could be relevant to solve the issue. Of great importance, though, is article 8, which takes the party's objective as well as subjective intent into consideration. Simply put, if the parties intended that a disclaimer will limit the buyer's remedies then a court or tribunal will give effect to that intent. The advantage of the CISG in this case is that the matter does not rest on some legalistic issue, whether certain words or types of words are used, as it is the case in § 2-316 of the UCC,[275] but whether the parties either objectively or subjectively agreed that a disclaimer will govern the contractual relationship between buyer and seller. Such an approach again is in line with the focus of the CISG to give certainty to international trade and hence will contribute to a uniform approach.

D. Set-off and article 4

Just because the CISG does not cover a particular issue, such as set-off, it does not necessarily mean that that issue has become an issue of validity. Article 4 goes beyond validity. Article 4 specifically points out that it only covers aspects of formation of the contract and governs 'the rights and obligations of the seller and the buyer arising from such a contract'. Arguably, therefore, set-off is not a validity issue pursuant to article 4(a) but rather falls outside the scope of article 4. It forms part of another contract which has no direct link to the current one.

272 Hartnell (1993: 3).
273 Mather (2001: 162).
274 Mather (2001: 163).
275 Mather (2001: 162).

A Dutch court used the above arguments as a justification from rejecting a set-off claim to be governed by the CISG. The court noted:

> [t]he question whether this [set-off] can be considered concerns a subject that is not governed by the CISG. Therefore it must be resolved under [the applicable] domestic law.[276]

This case makes it perfectly clear that it is not the matter of set-off that is a problem but rather at what time of the dispute the matter is brought up. The same court also had to consider another set-off emanating from the same case. This set-off was allowed because it concerned an overcharging on an invoice which was part of the then current debate.[277] In the same manner, a court allowed a buyer to set-off the damages against the purchase price.[278]

However, there is another argument which should be considered. Courts and tribunals relied on the part of article 4 which states that the CISG is only concerned with the rights and obligations of the seller and buyer 'arising' from such a contract. The word 'arising' can be given a very narrow meaning, such as arising from the current disputed contract. But arguably, a debt, as a result of a judicial decree, also arises out of a contract. The only difference is that the debt is now liquidated. Why can it not be used to set-off against another debt which will be liquidated as well? In essence, a court is simply arguing that there is a gap that needs to be covered by municipal law. With a more expansive interpretation, the same result can be achieved, namely a debt is set-off against a current debt under dispute.

A counter argument is that the legislative history does not support such a view. Furthermore, another problem is that a court would need to inquire whether the set-off is a consequence of a dispute involving the CISG.

It is true to say that the legislative history does not support an expanded interpretation of the term 'arising from such a contract'. However, it must be remembered that every international trade dispute is subject to domestic law, as recourse to the rules of private international law is needed to fill gaps. What this book has shown is that partial uniformity can be achieved and an endeavour to 'tinker at the edges' will increase uniformity of application. The issue of set-off has the potential to do so.

E. Invalidity and illegality: a discussion

Article 4 cannot be discussed meaningfully without investigating the issues surrounding the possibility that a contract may be invalid due to illegality.

276 *P.T. Van den Heuvel v Santini Maglificio Sportivo de Santini*, District Court Arnhem (Netherlands), 25 February 1993 [http://cisgw3.law.pace.edu/cases/930225n1.html].

277 *P.T. Van den Heuvel v Santini Maglificio Sportivo de Santini*, District Court Arnhem (Netherlands), 25 February 1993 [http://cisgw3.law.pace.edu/cases/930225n1.html].

278 District Court Trier, 12 October 1995 [http://cisgw3.law.pace.edu/cases/951012g1.html].

Illegality and invalidity are interrelated, but not the same. Illegality is closely related to public policy of a country and will in many cases be tied to mandatory rules, which make a choice of laws rule inapplicable. Despite the fact that a choice of law would lead to the law of a particular forum because of strong public policy issues, a court would be forced to apply the forum law rather than the applicable foreign law.[279]

If a question of illegality is raised, which is not within the mandate of the CISG, there is no problem as to which law applies. However, the possibility may arise that mandatory law of a country will preclude the application of the clause within the CISG. This, in a sense, is already happening through the right of contracting states to declare reservations in the acceptance of the CISG. In such instances, uniformity is not guaranteed, as domestic law would regulate the issue, whereas in other countries, the uniform CISG laws would be applicable. This issue needs careful attention by courts. As today the tendency to look at the international jurisdiction is becoming prevalent, a court or tribunal must take great care to explain the reasons why a matter that is included in the regime of the CISG is excluded because of illegality or other policy reasons.

In these instances, the question of validity is not a uniform matter to be resolved on an international level. It rather needs a case-by-case proposition determined by a choice of law issue. The fact is that a particular term in a contract, depending on the choice of law rule, may be found illegal under the forum's mandatory laws, however perfectly legal it may be in the other country. It has been argued that in such cases the rule of validation should be adopted, that is, the choice of law rule of the country where the clause is legal should be adopted.[280] The problem in such a proposition lies with the jurisdictional issue. If jurisdiction is sought in a country which has a vested interest in the maintenance of mandatory public laws, such as antitrust legislation, it will apply its public policy, which may exclude the other forum as being applicable. If jurisdiction had been sought in the other country, the outcome would be different. It is hardly a uniform result, but rather a forum-shopping ploy depending on the plaintiff's intentions.

The question of default rule, as discussed in chapter 4, can arguably produce uniform results. The uniformity is not to be found in the decisions but in the application of a particular forum, namely the country that has the closest connection to the dispute. It would be the seller's country if articles 31 and 57 were applied. Again, a problem of illegality, which in some countries makes contracts invalid, points to problems in trying to achieve total uniformity. However, as this book has been trying to explain, even when total uniformity is not achievable, the CISG still has solutions embedded within its four corners, which will at least guarantee uniformity in approaching a trade dispute. This alone will contribute towards certainty, as forum shopping is as much as possible restricted. In the end, the important test as to the applicable law should be based

279 District Court Trier, 12 October 1995, p 202 [http://cisgw3.law.pace.edu/cases/951012g1.html].
280 Ibid., 203.

on an international standard of justice, which suggests that 'the foreign law must violate a fundamental principle of justice that the forum shares with most civilised nations'.[281] Considering that the CISG is a compromise and a political instrument which offends no one, the question of violating fundamental principles of justice would hardly exist, and hence, uniformity is maintained.

F. The question of validity

No doubt, article 4 challenges the unification process enshrined in article 7. What can be achieved is that article 4 is applied uniformly, which at least would create some certainty. However, article 4 is often quoted as being an example which illustrates the tension between uniform laws and domestic laws.[282] The problem is that the CISG first did not define 'validity'. It is understandable that such a definition is a nearly impossible task, as the question of what constitutes invalidity can vary between domestic systems. Arguably, therefore, the promoters of the CISG did include certain aspects of validity into the convention and, by necessity, left some out. This is confirmed by Kritzer, who, in his editorial analysis of article 4, identified six references which in some countries equate to questions of validity.[283]

However, the solution is not a perfect one, and as early as 1981, the shortcomings of the validity issue were recognised. Ziegel did comment that 'the exclusion of questions of validity from the reach of the CISG is... a debilitating if unavoidable weakness'.[284]

The problem of the unavoidable weakness is that the solution of an autonomous interpretation, that is, interpreting the CISG within its four corners, has been criticised as only offering a majority view and hence does not uniformly contribute towards an international sales law. The problem seems to be the public policy issues, which are arising only in one or a few states.[285] The answer to such criticism is to ask whether it is preferable to have a majority view based on the interpretation of the CISG or always exclude domestic remedies from the CISG as proposed by the displacement theory. Such an approach is not practical, as it would lead to uncertainty. Questions of validity, as previously noted, are diverse and can vary between systems and encourage forum shopping, which is not conducive to achieving uniformity.

It appears that often two matters are overlooked. First, the CISG always has put substance before a label. Honnold correctly stated that:

> the uniform rules should not be displaced merely because of the labels attached to various doctrines of domestic law.[286]

281 District Court Trier, 12 October 1995, p 207 [http://cisgw3.law.pace.edu/cases/951012g1.html].
282 Leyens (2003).
283 Annotated Text of the CISG [http://www.cisg.law.pace.edu/cisg/text/e-text-04.html].
284 Ziegel (1981).
285 Leyens (2003).
286 Honnold (1999: para 240).

Bonell also succinctly writes:

> even in the exceptional cases where terms or concepts were employed which are peculiar to a given national law, it was never intended to use them in their traditional meaning.[287]

To consider these views has never been more important than in the application of article 4(a). It shows that uniformity of application must not begin with labels given by domestic laws, but by the substance of the problem. This leads to the second point, namely the criticism of a four-corner approach to the effect that it 'displays a lack of flexibility in regards to matters of evolving public policy'.[288]

The point to remember is that by ratifying the CISG, a country has adopted the convention as part of its domestic laws. As such, no domestic law, even a mandatory one, can displace the CISG. Changes to the CISG are not subject to domestic parliamentary rules but would require an international conference, and hence, a new ratification of the amended convention would be required. Therefore, public policy considerations can only 'tinker around the edges' of the CISG. If a matter is governed by the CISG, it remains within the sphere of the CISG, despite any domestic legislation. If, as an example, the parol evidence rule would be declared mandatory, it would not displace article 8. However, public policy that takes on the mantle of validity is only allowable if it is not governed by the CISG. Hence, to argue that the CISG needs to be flexible in regards to evolving public policy is not a persuasive argument. It is not debated that some issues of validity are governed by the CISG and some are not. The problem is and will remain *where* the dividing line is to be drawn. Article 4(a) will embody for some time to come 'an uneasy and inconclusive truce line, along which skirmishes continue'.[289]

Uniformity can be achieved if the four-corner approach is taken by those interpreting the CISG, and jurisprudence will give guidance as to which issues are included and which are not. It certainly is a myth to suggest that uniformity on the aspect of validity can be achieved quickly. At best, it is a matter of time and will be assisted by a growing body of decided cases. One issue will be discussed to explain and elaborate on the above points, namely to shed some light on the common law question of mistake.

G. The question of mistake

The doctrine of mistake is one of the issues which will reveal a number of uncertainties, ambiguities and irregularities of the CISG, as a question of

287 Bianca and Bonell, (1987: 74).
288 See Leyens (2003) for a discussion of the various approaches.
289 Hartnell (1993: 74).

mistake raises the question of validity.[290] Therefore, it reinforces the urgency that harmonisation and uniformity is only achievable in international trade if instruments such as the CISG are properly understood and applied. The worst enemy of uniformity is and will always remain the homeward trend of interpreters. The approach to the choice of words, as required above, fits into the policy of uniform interpretation, as it views words not in a national but international context. It also overcomes the problem Honnold describes as literary 'deconstruction'.[291] Such considerations make the choice of words harder and require a special solution. The drafters of the CISG solved this particular problem and consciously 'rooted out words with domestic legal connotations in favour of non-legal earthy words to refer to physical acts'.[292]

With this view in mind, article 4 can be given its proper meaning, and many problems can be resolved. In the end, it is not the black letter law approach that will supply a desired answer but what is economically useful and just.

Mistake in itself is a misleading term, as it can mean different things to different people. If, as an example, a sale involves a mistake in relation to the quality of goods, article 35 of the CISG will solve this problem. Simply put, any mistake that involves the delivery of goods, which do not conform to the terms of the contract, is subject to the provisions of the CISG. The reason is that as the CISG provides for a damage-based remedial system, the buyer cannot circumvent the CISG by claiming mistake and hence declare the contract invalid.[293] That does not mean that all types of mistake are covered by the CISG, as some types of mistake invoke the principle of validity and are, hence, excluded from the CISG.

There are two important points to be made. First, just because a particular breach of a contract is founded on mistake it does not automatically invoke the principle of validity. Some types of mistake, such as mistake as to the quality of goods, are governed by the CISG.

The second problem is that validity is in many instances interpreted from a domestic point of view. This is demonstrated by the fact that once validity is mentioned, immediately article 4 is invoked, without any thought being given to the mandate of article 7(2). The problem appears that as soon as terms such as mistake, duress and fraud are mentioned, article 4 is invoked. This is not the correct approach. Article 7(2) is totally ignored, whereas it should be the starting point of any investigation. If article 7(2) is invoked, the first step is to examine whether the CISG supplies the relevant answer. If no solution is found, a label may be given to the problem, and it may be labelled as a problem of validity. But whether it is a problem of validity or not is not a question of the CISG but a domestic one. If the CISG does not cover a particular problem of mistake, domestic law can be used to solve the problem. The domestic law of the forum

290 Leyens (2003).
291 Honnold (1995: 1, fn 6).
292 Honnold (1995: 2).
293 Leyens (2003).

in question may call the issue one of validity, and hence, pursuant to article 4(a), it is excluded from the sphere of the CISG and must be dealt with by domestic law. This approach is reinforced by article 4 itself.

There are two important connections within the article, namely 'not concerned with' and 'expressly provided'. Two approaches have emanated from the wording of the article. First, the opinion has been advanced that because the CISG is 'not concerned with' validity domestic law is responsible to supply the relevant answers to such questions.[294] On the other hand, those who focus on the term 'except as otherwise expressly provided' specifically draw on article 7(2) to find the boundary where validity issues are included in the CISG, as opposed to those which are by necessity left to domestic law to be determined.[295]

Of significance is that article 4 first notes that 'unless otherwise provided' the CISG will prevail, and only further is the CISG not concerned with validity. Arguably, to suggest that 'the scope of the negative rule (not concerned with) is limited by the positive one'[296] is not false but also not totally correct either. It would be more appropriate to suggest that the positive rule (expressly provided) is limited by the negative rule which is in line with the intention of article 7(2).

The inevitable result is that uniformity is only achieved if all courts and tribunals understand and use article 7(2) correctly and are not starting the investigation from an ethnocentric base, that is, looking at validity first. Simply put, the interplay between the CISG and domestic law needs to be understood as meaning CISG first, domestic law second.

H. Mistake – the conceptual framework

The starting point for any discussion needs to be the realisation that the CISG demonstrates a progressive attempt 'to achieve a meaningful unification of the law on international sales transactions'.[297] Mistakes can eventuate in any stage of the life of a contract. However, following the broad classification of the CISG, a mistake can eventuate in the formation of the contract or in the actual sale of goods, which includes the delivery of goods, the conformity of goods, and the remedial scheme. Of interest are the formation stage and the performance stage of a contract.

It needs to be understood that there is no universally accepted understanding of the doctrine of mistake, though some common features are present in most legal systems. Most common law countries distinguish between common mistake, mutual mistake, and unilateral mistake. The Swiss Law of Obligation, to take a civil law example, knows four forms of mistake (*Irrtum*), a declaratory mistake (*Erklärungsirrtum*), mistake as to circumstances (*Motivirrtum*), a qualified mistake

294 See, e.g., Hartnell (1993: 72).
295 See, e.g., Honnold (1999).
296 Leyens (2003).
297 Leyens (2003).

as to circumstances (*Grundlagenirrtum*), and a mistake as to the calculation of the price (*Kalkulationsirrtum*).[298]

However, both systems agree that a mistake is, in essence, a wrong of defective evaluation of a part of the contract. In other words, there is no objectively or subjectively ascertainable meeting of the minds. What vary greatly between systems are the consequences which can flow from such a mistake. Harnell suggests that:

> the drafters purposefully 'intended article 4(a) to serve as a loophole which could stretch to fit the needs of each domestic legal system'.[299]

The problem with such an interpretation of the drafters' intention is that it can mislead interpreters of the convention. It is true to say that there must be some flexibility in any uniform text to accommodate mandatory laws of any domestic system. If that were not the case, many countries would find it difficult to ratify a convention which on difficult issues runs contrary to their domestic laws. There is no clearer example than mandatory laws. However, it must also be remembered that an accommodation of mandatory laws had to take place at the ratification stage and not at a later date. Article 92 of the CISG is very precise on that matter.

The above interpretation leaves the door open for courts and tribunals to 'stretch the loophole' and decide a difficult issue on mistake using their own domestic laws instead of fitting the problem to the solution of the CISG. It does little to uniformity if courts and tribunals seek refuge in their own laws instead of promoting a uniform approach.

A good example is the difference between Austrian and German law in relation to a mistake in relation to the conformity of goods. Under German law, damages can be claimed similar to the scheme outlined in the CISG. Under Austrian law, on the other hand, a mistake as to conformity would allow an aggrieved party to avoid the contract, hence, claim the contract to be invalid. Obviously, article 35 of the CISG puts these problems to rest, as in this instance, the solution is 'expressly provided in this Convention'.[300] There appears to be no controversy that recourse to domestic law in this instance is permissible. There should equally well be no controversy if the matter is slightly more difficult and a court would need to look to general principles instead of at a 'ready made rule' contained within one article.

I. Mistake – an analysis

Mistake, as pointed out above, is classified in various ways by different legal systems. The common law and civil laws do not attribute the same labels to the

298 Schwenzer (2000: 226 ff).
299 Hartnell (1993: 21).
300 Art. 4(a) CISG.

same types of mistakes. This book, therefore, will use a commonly accepted classification, namely mistakes in expression and mistakes in motive.[301]

I. Mistakes in expression

This type of mistake evolves, in essence, around cases where both parties are under a misunderstanding and are therefore at cross-purposes. In common law, this is referred to as a mutual mistake. A third party or a person equally situated would ordinarily not detect such a mistake.

The only article which could possibly be of assistance to resolve the matter within the CISG is article 8. However, this is not the case. Article 8 always presupposes that when the objective or subjective intent of the parties has to be established, the yardstick is the understanding of 'a reasonable person'. As indicated above, the reasonable person would not suspect that there is a mistake, and hence, an agreement was never reached because assent was never reached. The contract was never properly instituted, that is, formation of a contract is defective.

In these cases, domestic law needs to be invoked, which considers the contract either void or voidable. There is no problem as to achieving uniformity, as it appears clear that only domestic law can resolve these types of mistake and article 4 is properly invoked.

II. Mistakes in motive

This mistake has been commonly referred to as a mistake in the understanding of one party of a declaration made by the other party, such as identity of goods or contractual parties. Most importantly, had the mistaken party known of the real state of affairs, it would not have entered into the contract.[302] In common law, these types of mistake are referred to as common or also as unilateral mistake.

Mistake as to the other party is indeed very rare, as most contractual matters between business people do not focus on the identity of the party but rather on the goods. This matter is only of significance if the performance relies on personal skills, such as a commissioning of paintings. These cases again are defective in the formation of the contract and are outside the scope of the CISG, as again, the contract is not valid.

If a mistake as to the existence of the goods has been made, two approaches are possible. First, the common law approach, as indicated in *Couturier v Hastie*,[303] can be followed, declaring that the formation of the contract is defective and no contract came into existence. In this case, it will become a validity issue outside the

301 Also used by Leyens (2003).
302 Zweigert and Kötz (1998: 412).
303 (1852) 8 Ex 40; 155 ER 1250.

scope of the CISG. The second approach is to look at the general principle of risk allocation. In this context, articles 68 and 79(1) are relevant. *Couturier v Hastie* could also be validly resolved under the CISG, but with a different outcome.

The goods were in transit and, pursuant to article 68, the risk had passed to the buyer from the time of the conclusion of the contract. This situation is only changed if the seller was either aware of or ought to have known that the goods had been lost or damaged and he did not disclose this to the buyer. If a court followed article 68, the validity argument is not sustainable any more because a valid contract has been formed. The common law declares the contract invalid; hence, the seller bears the loss, but the CISG in a sense shifts the burden to the buyer. Arguably, the maxim 'caveat emptor' is alive and well in article 68. Article 79(1) protects the buyer, as it shifts the burden of proof back to the seller who can only avoid liability if he can show that the failure to perform was due to an impediment beyond his control. However, in the end, as the goods cannot be delivered, the seller will be in breach of the contract. Schlechtriem noted:

> [u]nder Uniform Sales Law, a contract to deliver goods that have already perished at the time of the conclusion is to be regarded as valid. The impossibility of the seller to deliver is a breach of his obligation which gives the buyer the appropriate remedies, but does not make the contract void as under an applicable domestic law.[304]

This example again illustrates the importance to read the CISG correctly, as any homeward trend would result in a wrong decision, leave alone contributing to a uniform application of the CISG.

J. Conclusion

These few examples are sufficient to highlight again the importance of following closely the mandate of article 7(2). The best approach is to read the CISG within its four corners; only if a matter is excluded or a gap exists, which cannot be filled by principles stated within the CISG, can recourse to domestic law be taken. Only a strict application of the CISG will bring about uniformity and consistency and hence predictability of outcome, which is so important in international trade. In the end, the matter seems to be clarified by the drafting history of the CISG where it can be elicited that the drafters did not exclude a case from the CISG just because it could be addressed by domestic mistake-based remedies.[305] It is safe to argue that most of the issues, which are excluded from the convention through article 4, can be left out 'without endangering the convention's primary purpose of achieving certainty and predictability through uniformity'.[306]

304 Schlechtriem (1991: 11).

305 Leyens (2003).

306 Hartnell (1993: 93).

Chapter 8

Transplantation of laws

A. Transplantation of uniform international law – facts or fiction?

I. Introduction

So far, this book has attempted to discuss general principles of concern, that is, areas where a contribution to uniformity could be improved. This chapter will specifically investigate the impact of the CISG on the creation of domestic commercial laws. It will focus on two recent law reforms, namely UCC article 2 and the German law of obligations in the Civil Code (*Bürgerliches Gesetzbuch*). Both domestic laws are of importance because they are examples of how the CISG, which is recognised as the most successful unification of commercial law, assists domestic laws in their revision processes.

Today, it is almost compulsory that any revision of a domestic code or introduction of new principles into a domestic system be based on comparative studies. A particular model or function is attached to uniform law. Domestic and international law are, so to speak, moving towards the creation of a uniform commercial law that is equally applicable to foreign and domestic litigants. The over-all aim would be to abolish the problem that a domestic conflict potentially has a different outcome to an international one, despite the facts being identical or the same.

The concept of fundamental breach is an excellent example of how a persuasive concept in a uniform law may influence domestic as well as international sets of rules: the UNIDROIT Principles[307] or the Principles of European Contract Law[308] have adopted a very similar solution.[309] The same is true for the European Directive of 1999 on certain aspects of the sale of consumer goods.[310] Furthermore, the

307 Art. 7.3.1 UP.

308 Art. 9:301 PECL.

309 On the influence of the CISG on UNIDROIT and PECL see, for example, Schlechtriem (2005: para 3 *et seq*).

310 Directive 1999/44/EC of the European Parliament and of the Council of 25 May 1999 on certain aspects of the sale of consumer goods and associated guarantees, Official Journal L 171, 07/07/1999 P. 0012–0016. On the influence of the CISG on the EU-Directive see, for example, Pfeiffer (2002: 24); Faber (1999: 418); Staudenmayer (1999: 2394 *et seq*).

OHADA (Organisation for the Harmonisation of Business Law in Africa), a union of 16 African states, has adopted a common sales law, which follows the CISG almost to the letter.[311] The German Civil Code (*Bürgerliches Gesetzbuch*) may serve as a recent example of a domestic sales law that has adopted this concept.[312]

A problem which needs to be addressed at the outset is the question of the standing of domestic law when it tracks the uniform law of the CISG. It is universally rejected that cases and material of domestic law tracking provisions of the CISG can be used to interpret the CISG. *Delchi Carrier SpA v Rotorex Corp*,[313] as an example, has been universally condemned by academics and courts as 'not getting it right'.

The question remains what standing a transplantation of a CISG article into domestic law has. The temptation is to allow domestic case law and material to assist interpretation of the CISG, as the domestic law originates from a common source, namely the CISG.[314] However, such a conclusion is not correct. The CISG might originally have influenced the drafting of a particular domestic provision, but the social context, that is, the rhetorical community, is not the same and hence the outcome is potentially not the same. The philosophical base on which the new transplanted article rests is different to the one of the CISG, with the consequence that even transplanted laws must be rejected to serve as guides in the interpretation of the CISG.

This said, it must be pointed out that transplantation of a uniform nature will contribute towards unification of laws in general. It would be trite to argue that

311 See the references in Magnus (2005: introduction para 2).

312 §§ 280, 281 and 323 BGB, which are the core provisions of the German default law (*Leistungsstörungsrecht*), have adopted the term 'breach of obligation' (*Pflichtverletzung*) as the general concept for all kinds of contractual breach. Like the CISG, the BGB has not completely abandoned the differentiation between various categories of breach of contract (this is particularly emphasised by Wilhelm (2004: 1055 *et seq*). For example, where performance has been made, though not properly, the remedies available to the aggrieved party are more restricted than where there has been no performance at all, § 281(1) BGB; Arts 49, 64 CISG. On the similarity between the CISG and the new BGB see, for example, Stadie and Nietzer (2002: 432 *et seq*). For further domestic laws applying the notion of fundamental breach or similar key concepts within the framework for avoidance or cancellation of the contract see the Scandinavian sales laws (§ 39 Norwegian Sale of Goods Act 1988; § 39 Finnish Sale of Goods Act 1987) and Art. 6: 265 of the Netherlands Wetboek.

313 [http://cisgw3.law.pace.edu/cases/951206u1.html].

314 Sometimes courts have stated that, when interpreting the CISG, one should also consider decisions based on national law where the wording of the CISG corresponds to provisions of the national sales law, even if the national law does not apply to the case at hand. However, the case law and other legal materials relating to another legal system may be consulted only insofar as certain terms or solutions are clearly influenced by this legal system (e.g. Art. 74, sentence 2 CISG contains the 'foreseeability doctrine' to reasonably narrow down damages; the 'foreseeability test' traces back to the Common Law doctrine established in *Hadley v Baxendale*, 9 Ex. 341, 156 Eng. Rep. 145 (1854). As to the quoting of domestic sales law within the frame of a CISG contract, see *Chicago Prime Packers, Inc v Northam Food Trading Co et al*, U.S. Dist Ct, N D Illinois, East Div, 29 May 2003, CISG-online 796.

because the laws are similar or even the same the outcome will be the same. However, what can be argued is that an interpretation of transplanted law should not be fundamentally different to outcomes which the same law achieves in the CISG. A narrowing of the gap between domestic and international laws has been achieved. Domestic law is exposed to principles of international law and it is safe to argue that differences would be minimal in outcomes.

II. Unification and transplantation

Recently, some important modernisations of domestic law have taken place. The most notable are the introduction of the new Chinese Contract law in 1999, the revision of article 2 UCC and, in 2002, the modernisation of the German law of Obligations within the BGB. This in itself is of no great concern within an international sales regime, but of significance is that in some – although not in all – circumstances the CISG has played an important part in the endeavour to change domestic sales laws.

Certainly, the merits of uniform laws are not universally accepted. Three risk factors are noted. First, uniform laws can increase the impact of inefficient rules; second, the risk of differences in interpretation can occur; and third, novelty in uniform law risks uncertainty in what the legal rule itself requires.[315]

At least as far as the CISG is concerned, the problem of inefficient laws appears to be theoretical in nature. It must be kept in mind that the diplomatic conference did not 'manufacture' new laws, but rather looked at time-tested general principles that were included into the CISG. The risk of differences in interpretation certainly is one of the teething problems of new uniform law. Any new law, whether domestic or international, will need 'bedding in'. The CISG now can rely on close to 2000 decisions, and a uniformity of application can be observed.

The third point needs some further elaboration and is investigated in this chapter, namely the risk of uncertainty when a novel law is introduced. The novel law in question is not individual rules as such within the CISG, but the CISG as a new international sales law.

The first point of debate is the assertion that a uniform law, by increasing the variance as compared to formerly applicable laws, raises uncertainty.[316] The fact is that uncertainty is merely a question of time. In common law, precedents can be overruled or distinguished. As soon as that happens, academic and judicial writing flourishes, and debates for or against the changes abound. After a 'bedding in' time, the discourse abates until new changes appear. As an illustration, the question of forum convenience shows that the debate about the difference between UK principles and Australian principles has not yet been resolved. Uncertainty still persists. However, in regard to negligence, the

315 Walt (1999: 672).
316 Walt (1999: 676).

principle contained in *Donoghue v Stevenson*[317] hardly raises an eyebrow, as it is well and truly an established principle. The same can be said in relation to the CISG. Certainly the first decisions in any country were in certain circumstances of doubtful utility. However, today a remarkable consistency can be detected if jurisprudence is studied and, hence, uncertainty is no serious threat, at least not more than is inherent in every living legal system.

A further point which has been raised is the fact that 'novelty in uniform law can create doubt...about the content of a legal rule'.[318] That is certainly the case if a uniform instrument introduces a rule, which indeed is novel. However, as this book has explained in various sections, the CISG is a consensual instrument, which is constructed with well-established legal principles. At best, the argument can be advanced that sections of remedies of a breach of contract, such as fundamental breach, are a novel approach and, hence, can create doubt. Again, the doubt or uncertainty is a question of time. As soon as enough jurisprudence has been established, at least a general trend can be detected which eventually will contribute towards uniformity. The above arguments suggesting that a uniform law contributes towards uncertainty are not sustainable as the same arguments can be used as soon as new domestic law is created or domestic law is changed. It is the nature of any law that it requires a 'bedding in' time in order to overcome initial uncertainty. Walt lists four examples to illustrate the point he is making, namely the problem of the lack of one single canonical text,[319] the presence of undefined terms, such as those found in article 4, the question of good faith, and the inconsistency in the CISG rules on formation of contracts.[320]

Arguably, all the criticism listed by Walt displays a lack of understanding of the CISG, specifically the assertion that there is no canonical text and that there are undefined terms in article 4.[321] As far as the official languages are concerned, the existence of several texts can be viewed as an advantage. It allows in cases of doubt to check on several languages as two languages in certain circumstances cannot be reconciled and do not supply a definitive answer. To use article 3(1), as Walt did, the particular issue here is that the buyer supplies a 'substantial' part of material. Walt came to the conclusion that the English word 'essential' and the French text '*une part essentielle*' can lead to different conclusions.

What is the meaning of substantial? The German text – which, although it does not constitute an authentic translation of the CISG, is deemed to be of excellent quality[322] – as well as the French translation of the CISG use the words

317 [1932] AC 562.
318 Walt (1999: 676).
319 See also the doubts expressed by Flechtner (1998: 187 *et seq*).
320 Walt (1999: 676–681).
321 Art. 4 has been dealt with in a previous chapter, see Chapter 6.
322 On the formulation of the German text of the CISG see Schlechtriem and Schwenzer (2004: 29).

'*wesentlich*', and '*une part essentielle*'. '*Wesentlich*' does not match exactly the French or English translation. It corresponds better with '*une part essentielle*' rather than the English term 'substantial'. It is not debated that substantial or essential can be used to translate '*wesentlich*'. Hence, to look at 'substantial', as found in article 3(1), the word essential must be kept in mind and may help to overcome any ambiguities, which may otherwise arise.

Considering that all meetings in Vienna were conducted in English or French, these languages should be given priority over other authentic texts, as they best represent the intentions of the representatives at the 1980 Diplomatic Conference.[323] Hence, looking at the above comparison between the English, French and German translations, the German would carry less weight than the other two (in particular since the German is no authentic CISG language). It must also be noted that even between the authentic translations of the CISG solutions to unclear meanings of words are difficult especially if differences, which are of a conceptual nature, need to be understood.

It is interesting to note comments made by academics in the early 1980s warning that 'there are significant problematic issues regarding the Convention and it would be of doubtful wisdom for the United States to adopt it in its present form'.[324] Rosett furthermore argues that by ratifying the convention there will be 'little possibility of returning to the existing flexible system of state law if the experiment proves unsatisfactory'.[325] However, it is argued – and this book has shown that unification is never perfect – that a workable solution has been found. Arguably, whether the CISG has been a successful uniform instrument in the end, unfortunately, depends on personal experiences and views. Rosett, after 20 years, has not shifted in his opinion, and he still argues that:

> There are simply too many pitfalls, booby traps and murky abysses, too many unpredictable lacunae not yet definitively settled by universally recognized judicial interpretation.[326]

Such comments can be levelled at any domestic system as well. Just one example will suffice to illustrate the point. Article 2-608(1) of the UCC, where the buyer has the right to revoke the acceptance, uses the words 'whose non-conformity substantially impairs its value to *him*'.[327] The reading of this article would suggest that a subjective approach should be taken. However, the courts have established a two-pronged test: one subjective, the other objective.[328] A plain reading does not suggest such dual approach.

323 Diedrich (1996: 318).
324 Rosett (1984: 445).
325 Rosett (1984: 448).
326 Rosett (1984: 360).
327 Emphasis by author.
328 Pauly (2000: 228).

To contrast the views of Rosett, the Singapore Government has now instructed that all its contracts must include the CISG as the governing law. A further point must be added. The CISG has been applied in China on many occasions when the Convention would not normally be expected to apply. These decisions span the years from 1993 to 2000. The parties were mainly from either Mainland China, Hong Kong, and on occasion from Japan, the Republic of Korea and the United Kingdom.[329] It would not be surprising if the decisions would be arbitral ones but many are court decisions. It could be argued that the courts were mistaken in applying a convention which is not applicable. However the simple argument is that as a choice of law was not present the court assumed the authority to apply a domestic law that best suits the circumstances, namely the CISG. The fact that Hong Kong is part of China did not deter the Chinese courts from viewing the contract as having an international element. It can only be assumed that in the circumstances the courts felt that the CISG is the most appropriate law.

The conclusion arguably is that in the end a personal choice must be made to either embrace a uniform international law or remain firmly planted within each individual domestic paddock. Such endeavour is now becoming more difficult, as many instruments, such as the UNIDROIT Principles, which are frequently used in arbitration and domestic transplantation, are 'borrowing' principles from the CISG.[330]

III. The modernisation of the BGB

The obvious conclusion is that the differences between domestic and international law are being slowly eroded and the two laws are being brought into line with each other. It would be premature to argue that great progress has been made, but of significance is that the process has started. It is an admission that the CISG has merits and is the obvious tool in the unification process.

The drafting committee saw its mandate in a broad sense, namely to look at comparative studies of foreign legal systems as the foundation to implement changes in domestic law.[331] As Rolland reports, one of the express goals was to look at the CISG and adopt ideas with the intention of unifying international and domestic sales laws.[332]

However, Schlechtriem reports that the modernisation – the first in almost 100 years – caused some controversy. He notes:

> What caused particular vociferous protest was the suspected tendency to forgo parts of the Roman law heritage as interpreted by the great scholars of

329 List supplied by Al Kritzer. Document in possession and on file of Author.

330 On the influence of the CISG on UNIDROIT and PECL see, for example, Schlechtriem (2005: n 3 *et seq*). On the influence of the CISG on the EU-Directive see, for example, Pfeiffer (2002: 24); Faber (1999: 418); Staudenmayer (1999: 2394 *et seq*).

331 Pauly (2000: 238).

332 Rolland (1992: 2380).

> the 19th century such as Friedrich Carl von Savigny, who has strongly influenced some of the foundations of the German Civil Code in general and the sales law especially, and instead to follow solutions on the UN-Convention on International Sales, which was regarded as being a Trojan horse of common law thinking.[333]

It is interesting to note that such criticism should have been expressed considering that German jurisprudence of the CISG in general is outstanding. The CISG has been recognised in German courts as an important law and applied correctly. However, the above noted protests do support some of the criticism as to uncertainty of uniform laws, as expressed by Walt.[334]

Of interest is the change of the basic concept of breach in German law. The new terminology of *Pflichtverletzung* is equivalent to the general concept of performance found not only in the CISG but also in the UNIDROIT Principles and the European Principles of Contract Law. Of interest are §§ 323 and 434 of the BGB, that is, the concept of fundamental breach and conformity of goods and third party claims.

IV. Fundamental breach

Many legal systems allow for an avoidance of the contract without the requirement that the breach be significant.[335]

Where the seller has the duty to deliver specific goods and these turn out to be non-conforming, the buyer can either declare[336] or judicially claim[337] the termination of the contract. The buyer has the choice between termination of the contract and reduction of the price. Under certain restrictions, he can raise a claim for (further) damages, and some legislations state also a right to subsequent improvement. What is palpable is that in particular the Civil Law, as a general rule,[338] does not require a certain standard of seriousness of the breach in order to grant the remedy of termination of the contract.[339] But also where the parties have agreed on generic goods, termination of the contract is a rather easily available option. The aggrieved party can set the other party an additional period of time within which it should perform. After this period has lapsed, the first party can avoid the contract.

The CISG has adopted a different concept. A contract can be avoided only where the breach amounts to certain seriousness. The question is to define the

333 Schlechtriem (2002: 2).

334 Walt (1999: 671ff).

335 § 323 BGB; Art. 107(2) OR; §§ 918, 920 Austrian Allgemeines bürgerliches Gesetzbuch; Art. 1184 French Code Civil; § 2–601(1) UCC; §§ 241, 237 Restatement 2d (Contracts).

336 OR; ABGB; BGB; Greek CC.

337 Code Civil (France).

338 BGB has changed now.

339 See, however, Art. 205(2) OR.

relevant level of seriousness. The CISG has encapsulated two models as to when a breach amounts to such seriousness as to justify a termination of the contract:

> The first model states the basic rule that termination of a contract is allowed only in cases of a fundamental breach as a general principle, thus leaving it to courts or additional provisions to elaborate on cases of fundamental breach. The second model is based on a general requirement that the obligee first has to set an additional period of time to allow the obligor a second chance. [It is unnecessary only in cases] of an obvious fundamental or incurable breach.[340]

One of the criticisms of the CISG has been the problem of defining the term fundamental breach. Especially terms such as 'substantial detriment' mentioned in article 25 CISG have caused some problems. However, it must also be recognised that article 49 CISG allows an additional period of time to either deliver the goods or fix any defects in cases where goods have been delivered. Pragmatically speaking, a buyer or seller of goods contemplating avoidance of contract would choose the setting of a *Nachfrist* unless the breach is so obvious or substantial that such an additional time is not necessary. Also from an economic point of view – as the aggrieved party has invested time and energy into the contract – the setting of a *Nachfrist* makes sense. Arguably, therefore, the adoption of principles, which can be found within the CISG but in a more pragmatic fashion, is not an improvement of the CISG but a transplantation giving force to what may be considered the practical effect of the CISG.

The *Nachfrist*-model has its roots in Germanic legal systems. As has been mentioned, the starting point was to leave it to the aggrieved buyer whether he chooses to avoid the contract or switches to another remedy. Article 107(2) of the Swiss Code of Obligations, §§ 918, 920 of the Austrian *Allgemeines Bürgerliches Gesetzbuch* provide that where the buyer has set an additional period of time within which the seller fails to perform the contract properly, the buyer may terminate the contract. It is not surprising that the German law of Obligation would have a similar provision.

The new § 323 BGB has been substantially rewritten and the language has also been simplified. Arguably, the influence of the CISG is detectable in this provision. Section 323(1) BGB combines the criteria set in article 49 of the CISG. An additional period of time can be granted not only in situations of non-delivery but also where the goods have been delivered but do not conform to the contract. This constitutes a sensible simplification and conforms to practical situations. As an example, if a buyer orders black shoes and the delivery is either not on time or the shoes are green the effect is the same. He cannot fulfil his obligations to his customers. The CISG and the German Code of Obligation give the aggrieved party the same remedy. The common law, on the other hand, has

340 Schlechtriem (2002).

no provision which reflects the CISG's position on the treatment of a fundamental breach. In English and Australian Common law, fundamental breach is merely used as a term and at best is used for the interpretation of exemption clauses, but not to determine whether a contract lives or dies.

Section 323(2) BGB allows the aggrieved party to dispense with the *Nachfrist* if the obligor refuses to perform or if other 'special circumstances' exist.[341] Furthermore, like the CISG, the BGB introduced special rules governing the restitution of goods in case of a fundamental breach where the performance or delivery of goods has taken place. In essence, the CISG has, arguably, influenced the modernisation of the German Law of Obligations and has contributed towards a harmonisation of laws in the area of avoidance of contract. The BGB in the drafting of § 323 has overcome an awkward situation, namely that the 'German court would face the same problem of defining fundamental breach in two different contexts, in the CISG and the BGB context.'[342] However, the drafting committee took note of a decision of the Bundesgerichtshoft[343] where the court noted that the rights of the seller and buyer under the CISG are different from the ones under the [old] concepts of the BGB. Arguably, overcoming such difficulties must have been one of the reasons to adopt a CISG principle into the drafting of § 323.

V. The UCC concepts of article 2

The UCC article 2 revisions process started in 1988, when the Permanent Editorial Board (PEB) of the UCC and the American Law instrument in conjunction with the National Conference of Commissioners on Uniform State Laws (NCCUSL) approved a study on article 2.[344] There has never been a desire to introduce a process of internationalisation into the scope of the project, despite the fact that serious consideration was given to the harmonisation of domestic and international law.[345]

The reason can be derived by merely examining the composition of the bodies which were entrusted with the revision of the code. State, federal and professional interests had to be merged to achieve the desired result. Considering the opposition of some academics to the ratification of the CISG, such an outcome is not surprising.

Murray suggested that the 'current Article 2 rejection of technical requirements not only should continue but should be enhanced to remove the remaining impediments'.[346] Such a view would arguably lead at least to the

341 Schlechtriem (2002).
342 Pauly (2000: 239).
343 BGH VIII ZR 159/94 (1995) NJW 2099.
344 Murray (1994: 1450 fn 13).
345 Pauly (2000: 240).
346 Murray (1994: 1452).

realisation that the CISG also has an aversion for terms that are technical and, hence, could be of value to assist in the revision of the UCC. 'In fact the 1997 draft explicitly cites these [international] sources, including the CISG and draws the revision section in contrast to them.'[347]

Professor Speidel, the Reporter for the revision project, stated that the partial reflection of not using the CISG as a model was the NCCUSL's historical ambivalence towards international commercial unification.[348] He noted already in an earlier article:

> To the extent that CISG is a compromise among legal traditions rather than a systematic response to the realities of international trade, care should be taken in conforming domestic sales law to its provisions. This is especially true for Art. 2, since it is part of an integrated and uniform commercial code and is reasonably well adapted to modern domestic contracts for the sale of goods.[349]

This alludes to much criticism and perhaps a reluctance to embrace the CISG by suggesting that the convention suffers from an absence of compatible background law and article 2 is a part of an integrated commercial code.[350]

This is not the case, as the CISG, in essence, is based on general legal principles, which are common to most legal systems. It is true to say that some principles are closer aligned with either common law or civil law. However, this argument also holds true if some domestic legal systems are compared. Compatibility is not unique to international uniform laws. Furthermore, the CISG has a rhetorical community and, hence, has a compatible background law based on international jurisprudence.

Pauly made an interesting observation, and it may reflect the true nature of international law if measured against domestic legal systems.

> The process of unification of commercial law will be mainly inspired by scholarly opinions and the development of trade usages. It is interesting to note that more consent can be achieved this way than in congress, where diplomatic considerations dominate underlying common commercial and legal issues.[351]

To put the above discussion into context, one factor does emerge, namely unification is only achievable if national judges and national legal professions are taught to reverse their ethnocentric approach and understand that unification is a fact and not a myth.

347 Pauly (2000: 240).
348 Speidel (1995: 169).
349 Speidel (1993: 139).
350 Speidel (1995: 175–177).
351 Pauly (2000: 243).

However, the most important factors that influenced the drafters of the revision of article 2 were technical in nature. The mandate simply was to revise the sales provisions, not to draft a new commercial code. The aim was to bring the code up to date with modern business practices and reflect the current state of legal thinking.

As the UCC needs to be adopted by each state – and has been adopted in some form in 49 states[352] – a revision, therefore, will attempt to keep it that way, and therefore, the focus is on the domestic legal landscape and not the international one. This philosophical stance is reinforced by the fact that the CISG is a blend of common and civil law. There is doubt whether the drafters of a domestic commercial code, which in effect needs to be ratified by 50 states, would abandon common law principles in favour of a mix or even a predominantly civil law principle. As an example, article 8 of the CISG clearly denotes that the convention does not have a parol evidence rule, which in common law is the cornerstone of defining the content of a contract.

I. Fundamental breach

Between the CISG and the UCC, several structural differences exist and one of these concerns the buyer's rights in case of delivery of non-conforming goods. Under the UCC, the buyer can choose between accepting or rejecting the goods whenever the tender of delivery fails in any respect to conform to the contract § 2–601(1). Under article 49 and 25 of the CISG, a rejection of the goods is only possible if the buyer can show that the seller committed a fundamental breach. In essence, the CISG only allows for a termination of a contract in cases of a fundamental breach. For that matter, many common law countries rely on the law of warranty, which is unknown in the CISG. This, however, does not mean that the standard of conformity between the two systems is different. Indeed, they are virtually the same and the difference is only one of terminology.

Simply put, the standards for avoiding a contract affect the remedial structure of the two regimes. As the remedial structure is a crucial element of any legal system, it is understandable that the CISG was not taken into consideration when the UCC was revised and not redrafted. However, it is important to acknowledge that many rules that are present in the revised draft are consistent with the approach of the CISG, but they were not chosen because they are in the CISG. The choice was due to the fact that they evolved with common business practices.

What conclusions can be drawn? First, it does not indicate that the CISG is not a relevant sales regime. It indicates that, within a jurisdiction, law makers must be attuned to their own constituency, specifically when state and federal players must in the end agree on a result. It is entirely different if a legal dispute

352 Louisiana has not adopted the UCC in its present form.

spans two jurisdictions. The CISG assists in this instance, as each of the two jurisdictions can say that the dispute is solved by their 'own' sales law and not by a foreign one.[353] The reason is that the CISG is part of domestic law. The advantage of having the same sales law in all jurisdictions is obvious to see. However, the time is not ripe to see all regions and modernisations of law adopt the CISG. It no doubt will be a creeping transplantation though it is encouraging to note that principles in the UCC are basically consistent with the approach taken by the CISG. However, as also pointed out above, certain principles, such as fundamental breach, have no counterpart in many jurisdictions and will remain a point of contention in modernisation efforts.

B. Conclusion

The argument has been advanced that a new law 'containing highly general and open-ended terms creates uncertainty…and the crucial missing resource is supporting case law and more generally, precedent'.[354] Such criticism was certainly true in the beginning. But this is not only true for unified international law but novel domestic law as well. Any law which is new or novel needs to have a case history to support interpretation of any terms, whether they be open ended or clear and precise. The point is: it depends which interpretative tool is used. If the literal rule is used, the outcome is different from the purposive approach. As an example, a 'Street Offences Act' contains the rule that 'it is an offence to solicit in the street'. If the soliciting would be from a balcony, the solution depends on the approach. Using the literal approach, no offense has taken place, because the soliciting does not take place in the street. However, if the purposive approach is taken, then the 'street' is not to be interpreted literally but with the view of what the act intends to achieve, and hence an offense has occurred.

It has been correctly stated that only supporting case law and precedent will give necessary answers. This now has happened in the CISG and many decisions, such as the Court of Vigevano[355] and others who used existing foreign case law to guide them. It is therefore wrong to argue that:

> Novel uniform international sales law is unlike prominent uniform domestic sales law. Article 2 [of the UCC] developed a rich case law around it.[356]

The CISG has also developed a rich case law around it. As pointed out above uniformity is merely a question of time and it is trite to argue that 'only [the] hapless tend to have their contract governed by the CISG'.[357] On the contrary,

353 See De Ly (2005a: 36 *et seq*); Herbel (1999: 11).
354 Walt (1999: 681).
355 [http://cisgw3.law.pace.edu/cases/000712i3.html].
356 Walt (1999: 681).
357 Walt (1999: 688).

the hapless ones are those who get caught in a law that they do not understand and which is foreign to their thinking. The reluctance to apply the CISG is not a problem of its drafting but rather the reluctance of legal counsel to explain the advantages to their clients.[358]

It is interesting to note that German modernisation has looked at the CISG closely and in a sense aligned itself with the uniform sales law. The U.S. experience, on the other hand, is contrary to the German one. Perhaps the political climate and political constraints explain the different approaches of the two domestic systems.

Practical examples and the legal literature in a sense move between two extremes, namely that uniform law is a good thing or that uniformity is a myth. As this book has pointed out, the transitional stage has not been taken sufficiently into consideration. In other words, between the birth of a uniform law and its full implementation transitional problems will cloud the usefulness of a uniform law.

Not only transition of time is of importance but also the transition in commercial law needs to be taken into consideration. This chapter has indicated that a transition necessitates either the possibility that the law can adapt or that new laws are written.

The German experience has indicated that a revision or modernisation ought to take note not only of domestic needs but also of international models. In contrast, the U.S. experience did look at international uniform laws but the political climate was not conducive to include principles of the CISG into domestic law reforms.

Where from here? Arguably, the CISG has the potential to move further along the continuum of uniformity but 'learning externalities associated with novel terms are an important constraint on contracting parties' adoption of new uniform sales law'.[359] As it is anecdotally known, many legal advisors, mainly of big companies, advise their clients to exclude the CISG. No doubt such advice will change over time, as the new generation of lawyers is well aware of and fully acquainted with the CISG. The simple fact is that a novel approach, such as fundamental breach, is a 'collective action problem', which will be resolved over time and enhance the value of remedial actions for aggrieved parties.

The conclusion which can be drawn is that attention must be directed to perceive impediments which will in a given time frame detract from the optimal use of the CISG.

358 Magnus (1999: 25); Martiny (2001: 140); Kieninger (2002: 288 *et seq*); De Ly (2005a: 29); Ferrari (2002b: 737); see also Berger, Dubberstein, Lehmann and Petzold, (2002: 15, 34) with regard to CISG and other 'transnational law'.

359 Walt (1999: 704).

Chapter 9

Conclusion

A. Introduction

This book has attempted to demonstrate that the CISG has successfully unified international sales laws and has been the most successful international document so far. As Hartnell suggested, 'unification of the law governing the international sale of goods is an exercise in reconciling the necessary with the possible'.[360] However, at the beginning of the unification process the question must be asked: what are we aiming for? Sautet answered that question in the following fashion:

> The fact that pessimists are wrong does not prove that optimists are right. To describe the future of our civilization as a return to barbarity could be nonsense. However, that does not at all justify the undisputed reign of market laws over the destiny of humanity.[361]

We have moved from a modernist world to what might be called a postmodernist world. It is an undisputed fact that the absolute sovereignty of states over international transactions has ceased. International instruments are on the rise and a new and much wider rhetorical community requires legal certainty in its dealings. Knowing what we are aiming at requires that 'we suspend judgment for an instant while we review what we have been and where we are'.[362] This book has attempted to do so albeit in a limited way. Only certain critical or controversial issues have been examined and some conclusions as to the state of advancement have been made.

In order to be of practical value, a 'rule of law' of uniform law has to be established. It is the norm within uniform law. The problem is whether the CISG has been treated like any other domestic rule of law or whether the advantages of a supranational rule of law have been recognised. The advantage of the CISG is that it has state legitimacy and contains its own values in establishing its own legitimacy.[363]

360 Hartnell (1993: 93).
361 Sautet (1995: 15).
362 Marquis (2005: 2).
363 Marquis (2005: 50).

B. Where are we now?

Of immense assistance in this evolutionary process is the fact that tribunals and courts around the world have access to databases regarding the CISG, which unifies a community of people around the text of the Convention.[364] Cook suggested that:

> There is little hesitation to embrace CISG as a solid compromise position if the application of the U.C.C is not available.[365]

After 17 years, the growth of the material that is available on websites is striking and the 'uniformity of cases from many jurisdictions suggests a high awareness of each other's work'.[366]

Kastely in 1988 already foresaw the importance of such a development when she wrote:

> What is called for, in essence, is the development of a jurisprudence of international trade. This is the heart of the rhetorical aspiration [of the CISG]. Its success directly depends on the achievement of this goal.[367]

Arguably, this goal has been achieved and the CISG has succeeded to form the basis of a unified international sales law.

The CISG has also influenced domestic law and has been used as a model for reform. Most importantly, the Convention has influenced the drafting of the EC Directive convening the sale of consumer goods.[368] This is significant, as the CISG specifically excludes consumer contracts from its sphere of influence pursuant to article 2. As such, the EC Directive is not a product of primarily copying existing rules and regulations but an adoption of principles and, hence, an awareness that the underpinning philosophical structure of the CISG is well suited to serve today's commerce. Furthermore, the influence of the CISG is also noticeable in the Unified Business Law Act drawn up by the OHADA group of African nations. The drafters relied heavily on the provisions of the CISG in the creation of general commercial law that is contained in the OHADA document.[369] Moreover, influence of the CISG on Europeanisation approaches can also be detected noticeably in the drafting of the Principles of European Contract Law, which in turn greatly influenced the development of a unified contract law in the EU.

364 Charters (2005: 13).
365 Cook (1998: 353).
366 Charters (2005: 14).
367 Kastely (1988: 600–601).
368 Kruisinga (2004: 10).
369 Kruisinga (2004: 11).

Interestingly, despite European attempts to harmonise the divergent national contract laws existing within Europe, many interest groups feel that this is not of great importance. The manufacturing industry in their submission to the Commission noted:

> differences in national legislation do not represent a significant obstacle to cross-border transactions because in most cases private international laws, the Convention on the International Sale of Goods (CISG) and existing Community law provide satisfactory solutions.[370]

The business community in the EU responded to the suggestion which seeks to create a coherent contract law indicating that the CISG provides a satisfactory conclusion. The conclusion which arguably can be reached is that uniformity has been achieved.

At the same time it must also be said that the CISG is by no means a perfect tool and total unification has not been achieved. Such a goal would be illusionary, as the harmonisation attempt is driven by political forces, which by necessity will result in a document that is in essence a compromise.

There are basically three problems that are not conducive to a uniform approach. The first two problems are within the CISG, the third one unfortunately goes beyond the convention and is a matter of concern. The first problem is how the inevitable gaps are to be filled. Second, the interpretation of the articles of the Convention have not always been in a uniform fashion. However, as far as practicable, this has been overcome with the help of an international jurisprudence. By far the greatest obstacle to uniformity is not the Convention itself but the inability of courts and the legal profession to abandon the ethnocentric approach to international documents. The inability of some courts, tribunals and the legal profession to lift their feet out of the domestic paddock has hindered the unification process of international sales laws, not only in its recognition but also in its application.

The terms of the Convention have been misconstrued and misapplied in many countries, but nowhere as blatantly as in Australia, Canada and the United States. In most other countries – and this is expected – some bad decisions have also been made. In most cases, however, other courts in the same hierarchy or in other jurisdictions have commented on and corrected the disputed decisions. For example, there are the earlier Italian decisions on article 1(1)(a), where a reference to a country's laws in a conflict of laws clause, such as 'the law of Italy will apply', has been interpreted as excluding the CISG. This interpretation is now universally discredited.

370 Communication from the Commission to the European Parliament and the Council, A more Coherent European Contract Law, an Action Plan, Official Journal of the European Union 2003/63/1–44, p 22.

C. Uniformity – critical comments

Besides simply not applying the CISG correctly, there have also been the inevitable critical comments. The argument has been advanced that the CISG is not delivering uniformity, that, to the contrary, the Convention is an obstacle to uniformity. The thrust of the argument is that the Convention has misguided goals. Furthermore, due to its character as a multinational treaty, its specific provisions will never allow the CISG to lay claim to be a uniform instrument.[371] Furthermore – and this criticism is relevant to the United States only – the CISG has been incorporated into U.S. law as a self-executing treaty.

The solution that has been offered falls into three categories, namely U.S. federal legislation, UNCITRAL review of all court decisions involving the CISG and a broad interpretative approach by courts when called upon to apply the CISG.[372] None of these solutions are either new or offer any substantive advancement in further harmonising the application of the CISG.

The second point of the offered solution in relation to a commentary generated by UNCITRAL is misguided. It would be inappropriate for UNCITRAL to make any announcements as to case law, as it is left to domestic courts to interpret their own laws. After all, the CISG, as enacted into domestic legislation, has become part of domestic law and it is left to domestic courts to give meaning to their own pieces of legislation. For UNCITRAL, to interfere with this process would not be tolerated. At least courts of different legal systems are accorded persuasive standing but UNCITRAL could not aspire to be given that particular standing. Furthermore, UNCITRAL, being a body of the United Nations, would be politically prevented from making statements of this kind.

It appears obvious that U.S. federal legislation in any shape or form would not affect the uniform character of the CISG. It is merely a domestic move to bring the CISG into a particular domestic legislative framework which is, in any case, a domestic matter and does not affect the international application of the CISG at all.

The further assertion of Bailey that the CISG as a self-executing treaty makes parties unaware of its existence and hence fosters disharmony based on ignorance of its existence is false.[373] Such an argument appears to suggest that ignorance of the law is an excuse, which has never been accepted in any court. Any legal practitioner worth his weight ought to know by now that international conventions are being drafted and ratified at regular intervals and a glance into any law journal would make even a casual observer aware of the CISG. It ought to be obvious to check for new legislation. Furthermore, in

371 Bailey (1999: 276).
372 Bailey (1999: 276).
373 Bailey (1999: 284).

Australia, the CISG was adopted by each state parliament as the Sale of Goods (Vienna Convention) Act. The problem of ignorance and misapplication are the same as in the United States. For that reason alone to suggest that it is because of the self-executing character that attorneys are unaware of the CISG is trite. More to the point, the old saying that 'you cannot teach an old dog a new trick' would be more appropriate in this instance.

Another argument must be addressed, which causes some problems in relation to a uniform approach to the CISG, namely the declarations of reservations. This issue is recognised as not fostering a uniform approach in the application of the CISG. However, as indicated above, some problems are unavoidable. It must be pointed out that information in relation to reservations is freely available and any research of litigating parties will reveal this problem.

Another point of concern mainly in the United States is the fact that a federal law which is enacted and is in conflict with the CISG will override the Convention. This has been expressed in *Reid v Covert* where the court held that

> when a statute which is subsequent in time is inconsistent with a treaty, the statute to the extent of the conflict renders the treaty null.[374]

It is possible that the Congress could pass a law which could, taking the last shot doctrine into consideration, be inconsistent with the CISG. It is common knowledge that a convention – and the CISG is no exception – can only be amended by a protocol after a diplomatic conference. It would be strange indeed that the UCC Commissioners would not realise this problem, especially considering that some Commissioners are law professors and well versed in the CISG. Though the theoretical framework exists, there is real doubt that such an occurance will eventuate.[375] So far, in most countries the opposite applies. In Australia, as an example, the introduction of the CISG found that the statute of fraud was incompatible with the CISG and therefore was changed to bring it in line with the Convention, and not the other way around.[376]

D. The problem of interpretation

The CISG, unlike other conventions, has introduced interpretative articles, namely articles 7 and 8. These articles, particularly article 7, have attracted some negative comments. Compared to domestic law, article 7 is not precise but relies on general principles. However, it must be pointed out that much academic writing has explained the function and content of article 7 and not much

374 354 U.S. 1, 18 (1957).

375 As an example, Professor Gabriel from Loyola University, New Orleans, who published widely on the CISG, is a Commissioner. He indicated strongly – in private conversations – that such a conflict would simply not eventuate, as, politically, such a course of action would be resisted.

376 Khoury (1990).

divergence can be detected.[377] Still, two types of criticism persist and must be addressed. The first point is that the CISG as a whole has no history, and second, the articles themselves have no substance and are not precise enough.

It has been said that the CISG

> is a piece of dislocated uniform law fed by diplomatic compromise and denied knowledge of its progenitors. It rests upon no particular legal culture and depends upon a country's private international law rules for its associations. In contrast the United Kingdom Sale of Goods Act 1979 floats in a sea of contract and personal property law.[378]

Several comments are necessary. First despite the criticism of the CISG it is still recognised as being a uniform law. The fact that possibly it has no knowledge of its progenitors does little to change the fact that it is a uniform law. Uniformity is not a matter of ancestry not legal culture. It simply rests on the fact that it is applied by a vast number of courts and that it reaches beyond state borders. A distinction needs to be made between an interpretation and a governing substantive law. As an example, if an Italian exporter sends goods to Germany, Australia and Switzerland he knows that his transactions will be governed by the same law, namely the CISG. Uniformity is achieved. Whether the application and hence interpretation displays the same uniformity is another matter. Unfortunately it gives rise to another argument. Indeed it has to be admitted that total uniformity is not achievable, as this book has shown. However, it can be argued that taking a global view of uniformity is achievable and enough jurisprudence is available to demonstrate this fact.

Another point to note is that the CISG also 'floats in a sea of contract and personal property law'. There are two important facets to the CISG: first it relies on general principles that are universal in character, that is they are found in most if not all legal systems. In other words, the CISG relies on uniformly acceptable legal principles. As the convention is applied by municipal courts any gaps can be filled by municipal law hence it rests not only on general principles but where no solution is offered the domestic law with all its history will supply the answer. In a sense, if all concerned know exactly how a law will be applied, uniformity of application is achieved.

Another very important feature giving the CISG 'knowledge of its progenitors' can be found in the debates of the CISG leading up to the adopting of the Convention. Not only did the developed world such as the United States play an important role, but so did the developing nations, many of whom were

377 For example, see Van Alstine, M, Dynamic Treaty Interpretation 146 University of Pennsylvania Law Review (1998) 687–793; Baasch-Andersen (1998); Ferrari, F , Tribunale di Vigevano: Tribunale di Vigevano Specific Aspects of the CISG Uniformly Dealt With 20 Journal of Law and Commerce (Spring 2001) 225–239.

378 Bridge (1997: 283).

absent in the previous attempts at unification. The end result was a 'political compromise [resulting in a] balance of interests between developing and developed world, suppliers of manufactured goods and suppliers of natural commodities, north and south...with little separating the above interests'.[379] Arguably therefore ownership in the CISG can be claimed by many interest groups and legal systems, hence a familiarity with the provisions of the CISG should be guaranteed.

Another feature which makes an application of uniform laws easier is the fact that court decisions are reported regularly, kept at one depository and are also regularly translated into English.[380] Cross-citation from diverse jurisdictions has become an easy matter and is not an impediment to uniformity any more.

E. Article 7 and the mandate of uniform interpretation

The principle of interpretation in the end will need to focus on article 7. Arguments have been advanced that the principles embodied in article 7 have failed to guide national courts to a consistent interpretation of the treaty.[381] The problem with such a view is that the purpose of article 7 has not been grasped fully. Article 7(1) explains how the interpretation of the individual articles of the CISG must be approached. The first criteria, namely the international character of the Convention alerts the courts and tribunals to the fact that ethnocentric views have no place within the CISG. The need to promote uniformity as the second criteria is an extension of the first criteria and good faith is the 'glue' which holds the interpretive mandate together. In other words the interpretation of the CISG is to be done within its fours corners, without recourse to domestic principles and with an eye on international jurisprudence. There is no mystery in article 7(1); it is a straightforward reminder to courts and tribunals that, despite the fact that the CISG is applied by national courts, national principles cannot impinge on the decision which emanates from the CISG. There is no further need to say more. It is difficult to see how article 7 is 'vague and difficult to apply'.[382] If as an example the Warsaw Convention is analysed, no interpretational aid is accorded to that convention. The only aid to interpretation is the *travaux préparatoires* and the Law of Treaties, namely articles 31 to 33. There is no substantive literature suggesting that the Warsaw Convention is vague and difficult to apply. Even the problem of defining 'accident' pursuant to article 27 of the Warsaw Convention has been solved by taking recourse to international jurisprudence.[383] The Domestic Courts went even further by

379 Bridge (1997: 283).

380 Pace website [http://www.cisg.law.pace.edu/].

381 Bailey (1999: 286).

382 Bailey (1999: 287).

383 As an example see *Povey v Qantas Airways Ltd.* (2005) 79 ALJR 1215.

suggesting that Australian law when borrowed from International Conventions must be interpreted in line with international jurisprudence.[384]

The point is that any article of the CISG must be looked at on its own merits as in the end facts will decide decisions. As an example, article 39 notes that the goods must be examined and notice of any lack of conformity must be given to the seller 'within a reasonable time'. The problem is what is a reasonable time? First it depends on the facts. There is no mystery that if perishable goods are concerned the time is very short and if the problem concerns manufactured goods, which are on-sold without the buyer actually receiving the goods, the time is longer. Article 7 will not supply the answer at all. What article 7 will do is ensure that the courts and tribunals cannot resort to domestic principles and that international jurisprudence ought to be consulted in coming to a decision. To arrive at a broad outcome article 7 is not required, but the 'fine-tuning' is regulated by broad principles contained within article 7. The outcome is that the timeframe is short and hence a uniform application of the CISG has been achieved. Whether one court allows three days and another court of a different jurisdiction allows five days is of no consequence as far as the goal of uniformity is concerned. Again article 7 assists: because of the 'international character' of the dispute, quick decisions need to be made and certainty and speed are required to minimise the costs of international trade. The most important aspect in solving any controversy in the application of uniform laws is the lack of understanding of its international character.

F. The international character of the CISG

I. The problem of internationality

The international character of the Convention and the observance of good faith dictate a policy of avoiding the application of domestic law. This is very important especially in the case of Australia and the United States where domestic legislation tracks in part the CISG. In *Filanto S.p.A. v Chilewich International Corp* (*Filanto*),[385] the court acknowledged this but made the following remarks:

> [the Uniform Commercial Code] does not apply to this case, because the State Department undertook to fix something that was not broken by helping to create the Sale of Goods Convention which varies from the Uniform Commercial Code in many significant ways.[386]

384 See for further illustration, *Uniform Law Review* 4 (2005), *Air Link Pty Ltd v Paterson* , 908.
385 United States, 14 April 1992 U.S. Dist.Ct. [http://cisgw3.law.pace.edu/cases/920414u1.html].
386 United States, 14 April 1992 U.S. Dist.Ct. [http://cisgw3.law.pace.edu/cases/920414u1.html].

The court importantly recognised that the CISG and the UCC are not interchangeable but missed the real significance of the CISG to respond to the international need of a uniform sales law. However *Filanto* did establish that there should be no room left to apply 'functionally equivalent, but differently construed national rules'.[387] The temptation for judges and the parties settling disputes is to look at what is familiar, especially at first glance. For example in *Calzaturificio Claudia S.n.c. v Olivieri Footwear Ltd* (*Calzaturificio*),[388] the judge commented that:

> ...case law interpreting article 2 of the Uniform Commercial Code may also be used to interpret the CISG where the provisions in each statute contain similar language.[389]

Such attitudes are not restricted to American CISG jurisprudence alone. In *Kotsambasis v Singapore Airlines Ltd*,[390] the court referred to *The Shipping Corporation of India Ltd v Gamlen Chemical Co*.[391]

> It is only if the interpretation of certain words by a national court assists in the interpretation of the same words that appear in an international Convention that any significant weight can be imported to the municipal law.[392]

To solve issues within the CISG – or any Convention for that matter – by analogy with domestic law is contrary to the international character.

As an example, in Australian law, § 19 of the Goods Act (Vic) 1958, tracks article 35 of the CISG. Great care needs to be taken that interpretation of the CISG is not attempted with the language or case law of § 19 in mind, specially if there is little international case law to guide the court. In *Delchi Carrier SpA v Roterex Corp* (*Rotorex*),[393] the judge recognised that there is virtually no case law under the Convention. He then pointed out that in such a case, 'we look to its language and to the general principles upon which it is based'.[394] The court appeared to recognise the importance of avoiding the

387 United States, 14 April 1992 U.S. Dist.Ct. [http://cisgw3.law.pace.edu/cases/920414u1.html].

388 United States, 6 April 1998 Federal District Court [New York], 96 Civ. 8052 (HB)(THK) 1998 [http://cisgw3.law.pace.edu/cases/980406u1.html] 2.

389 United States, 6 April 1998 Federal District Court [New York], 96 Civ. 8052 (HB)(THK) 1998 [http://cisgw3.law.pace.edu/cases/980406u1.html] 2.

390 Matter No CA 40154/96 (13 August 1997) [http://www.austlii.edu.au].

391 [1980] 147 CLR 142.

392 [1980] 147 CLR 159.

393 U.S. Circuit Court of Appeals (2nd. Cir) 6 December 1995 [http://cisgw3.law.pace.edu/cases/951206u1.html].

394 U.S. Circuit Court of Appeals (2nd. Cir) 6 December 1995 [http://cisgw3.law.pace.edu/cases/951206u1.html].

application of domestic law by pointing to the fact that 'the Convention directs that its interpretation be informed by its international character'.[395] Despite the fact that *Rotorex* understood the mandate of article 7, the court went on to proclaim that: 'Case law interpreting analogous provisions of article 2 of the UCC may also inform a court where the language of the relevant CISG provisions tracks that of the UCC'.[396] In this respect, *Rotorex* made the same misinterpretation as the one in *Calzaturificio*, with the difference that in *Rotorex* the court, at least, recognised that 'UCC case law is not per se applicable'.[397] However, *Rotorex* went on to review exclusively UCC case law as an aid to interpret the CISG. *Rotorex* missed the point that article 7(1) sets the goal of the interpretation of the CISG.[398]

The first Canadian decisions in 1998 set a poor precedent for the application of the Convention. In *Nova Tool & Mold Inc v London Industries Inc* (*Nova Tool*),[399] the litigant as well as the judge ignored the CISG and applied domestic law, despite the fact that rightfully the CISG should have been applicable. The second Canadian case, *La San Guiseppe v Forti Moulding*,[400] is no less intriguing. The CISG was applied as the correct governing law. Swinton J. did apply the relevant articles but failed to recognise the implications of article 7. In a discussion where she states that the seller did not breach article 35 she added that the seller did not breach the §§ 14–16 of the Ontario Sale of Goods Act either.[401] It appears that Swinton J. was not aware of the mandate in article 7, which states that the CISG overrides domestic law. Domestic sales law cannot coexist with the provisions contained in the CISG. It also needs to be noted that in a further statement in the decision, § 121 (1) of the Courts of Justice Act was used to calculate pre-judgment interest where, in effect, article 78 in conjunction with article 74 governs the question of interest.

The failure of courts to correctly interpret and apply article 7 can be attributed to a failure to recognise that the method of interpretation still remains a textual one, with the addition that the purpose of the Convention, the legislative history and the drafters' intent may be taken into account.[402]

395 U.S. Circuit Court of Appeals (2nd. Cir) 6 December 1995 [http://cisgw3.law.pace.edu/cases/951206u1.html].
396 U.S. Circuit Court of Appeals (2nd. Cir) 6 December 1995 [http://cisgw3.law.pace.edu/cases/951206u1.html].
397 U.S. Circuit Court of Appeals (2nd. Cir) 6 December 1995 [http://cisgw3.law.pace.edu/cases/951206u1.html].
398 Thiele (1998: 3).
399 [1998] O.J. No. 5381, 84 A.C.W.S. (3rd) 1089.
400 Canada, 31 August 1999 Ontario Superior Court of Justice [http://cisgw3.law.pace.edu/cases/990831c4.html].
401 Canada, 31 August 1999 Ontario Superior Court of Justice [http://cisgw3.law.pace.educases/990831c4.html].
402 Canada, 31 August 1999 Ontario Superior Court of Justice [http://cisgw3.law.pace.educases/990831c4.html].

Most importantly, the CISG cannot be interpreted from national juridical constructions and terms.[403] *Rotorex* mistakenly noted that

> The CISG requires that damages be limited by the familiar principle of foreseeability established in *Hadley v Baxendale*, 156 Eng. Rep. 145 (1854).[404]

The principle of foreseeability may well have been established in *Hadley v Baxendale* but it is based on a domestic concept. The principle of foreseeability may well coincide with the one expressed in article 74 of the CISG but to tie *Hadley v Baxendale* into article 74 is patently wrong.

Rotorex is a good example of the danger that domestic courts could construct the CISG within their own experience and procedures, especially where a court relies heavily on a literal interpretation and concludes that solutions must be found within the statute, as the only expression of parliament's wishes. The second danger lies in the choice of precedents. It is well established in Australia that precedents are only found within our own legal systems. Cases outside our body of law are regarded at best as persuasive but certainly not binding. The CISG breaks this particular view. To 'promote uniformity in its application',[405] the Convention indicates that the creation and application of precedents extend beyond national boundaries. Authority for such an approach is not only derived from the Convention but also from recent cases decided under the Warsaw Convention, specifically article 17.

II. Interpretation within the 'Four Corners'

There is a danger that some domestic tribunals, especially in countries that rely heavily on precedent, may 'take their eyes off the principles and engage in distinguishing, overruling and even manipulating precedents'.[406] Australian tribunals culturally try to find the answer within the statute itself, and treat cases outside their jurisdiction – if guidance is required – as secondary material. In *Roder Zelt- und Hallenkonstruktionen GmbH v Rosedown Park Pty Ltd et al*,[407] as an example, Von Doussa did not refer to either CISG case law or scholarly writings. He followed the suggestion of Hillman who maintains that tribunals should 'try to find answers within the "Four Corners" of the Convention and to look to cases only in the unusual case where the Convention does not supply adequate guidance'.[408]

403 Enderlein and Maskow (1992: 55).
404 *Rotorex*, above fn 393.
405 CISG, art. 7(1).
406 Hillman (1997).
407 [http://cisgw3.law.pace.edu/cases/950428a2.html].
408 Hillman (1997).

Such an extreme view is fraught with danger. It assumes that all tribunals understand the principles contained in the CISG as well as use the same method of interpretation. It also assumes that concepts expressed in the CISG are understood by all. Such an approach as advocated by Hillman can lead to fragmentation rather than uniformity. Cases are still the only international expression of an interpretation of the CISG by a domestic court. They indicate to other tribunals how a particular principle has been interpreted and applied. This is an important step in achieving uniformity.

Some examples will illustrate this point. The Obergericht Luzern[409] reviewed international case law to arrive at a determination of the terms 'examination of the goods'[410] and 'notice of lack of conformity'.[411] The court concluded that German case law interpreted the above cases narrowly whereas the Dutch and American indicate a more liberal approach. The court observed that the gap between these two positions had to be narrowed in order to arrive at a uniform application of the CISG.[412]

The Obergericht Luzern demonstrates that the approach advocated by Hillman will not lead to uniformity. Importantly, it will afford scholars the opportunity to critically analyse these decisions and if necessary point to errors. The first step is to look within the 'Four Corners' of the CISG. Second, courts need to consult cases and scholarly writings and treat them as persuasive. In this way the international character and the promotion of uniformity are guaranteed. Suggestions have been made that, as foreign decisions are not available or the court decisions are not expressed adequately, it is increasingly difficult to keep the code uniform.[413] Initially, it was difficult to obtain judgments, but the increased awareness of the CISG and the translation of important decisions into English increase the accessibility to a point where foreign decisions are as accessible as domestic ones. Arguably, though only decisions of superior courts are to be judicially consulted, decisions of inferior courts are of interest to academic writers and are an indication how much the CISG has penetrated the hierarchy of courts. Therefore, it would be difficult to keep the CISG uniform if we could not look to and consult foreign judgments.

The meaning of terms and rules has to be concluded from the words within the CISG. But a construction is not only reliant on the words but also the context and function the rules have within the CISG as well as other material, which has a connection to the CISG.[414] This point can be illustrated by re-examining a term confined to the common law system, namely, the parol evidence rule. The mere

409 Switzerland, 9 January 1997 [http://cisgw3.law.pace.edu/cases/970108s1.html].

410 CISG, above fn 1 art. 38(3).

411 CISG, above fn 1 art. 39(1).

412 Obergericht Luzern, above fn 409 CLOUT abstract no 192.

413 Keily (1999: 17).

414 Keily (1999: 17).

fact that this rule is confined to the common law system would, at first glance, bring it into conflict with 'the international character and uniformity of application' of the CISG. In *Calzaturificio*[415] the court recognised this by stating that:

> contracts governed by the CISG are freed from the limits of the parol evidence rule... [and] the standard UCC inquiry... has little meaning under the CISG.[416]

As a further example U.S. courts used 'naturally and normally' as a test to determine the application of this rule. Flechtner suggested that: 'The use of a test so firmly tied to our domestic law traditions without clear authorization in the text of the CISG would do violence to the directives of article 7(1).'[417]

In sum, this part has shown that the international character of the Convention demands that its interpretation is done without recourse to national laws. The above discussion has revealed several decisions where this mandate was not met. Put into perspective, it can be argued that since more than 1200 decisions were looked at, cases where recourse to domestic law has been taken are rare. They appear to emanate from early decisions within several jurisdictions but mainly from common law countries.

On the surface, the above cases would disprove the contention that the CISG is a uniform body of law. But put into perspective, only isolated cases can be found which do not fulfil the mandate of the 'international character' of the Convention. Additionally, these errors do not form a lasting pattern and are more likely 'teething problems' of the CISG within a domestic jurisdiction.

G. Conclusion

There is no better way to confirm that the CISG has developed into a truly international uniform law than through studies undertaken by academics on particular issues. Charters as an example studied article 8 and the influence this article exerts on article 35. Case studies have shown that the decisions are uniform and on the whole are not referring to domestic law. The situation is enhanced with the availability of a worldwide compilation of decided cases, which supports an institutional system of 'a community of CISG interpreters that, with or without citation acknowledges foreign decisions and has the recourses to interpret the CISG'.[418]

415 *Calzaturificio*, above fn 388.

416 *Calzaturificio*, above fn 388. It is interesting to note that, preceding the above statement, the court engaged in a detailed discussion documented with cases, on the parol evidence rule.

417 Flechtner (1995: 156).

418 Charters (2005: 41).

It is fitting to end with the conclusion Charters reached:

> The CISG is a compromise. As such, it is its own system capable of guiding decisions to enforce the system for a long time. The 'situational system' recognizes the market in a 'real world' form, compatible with the regulated markets of the world economy.[419]

The CISG is as close to a uniform instrument as it possibly can be. Arguably the CISG has now reached a point where it can be said that an institutional system supports the Convention. The institutional system is backed by the publication of decided international cases and most importantly the CISG can rely on its own community of interpreters, who bases their decisions on a real world of international trade. The greatest obstacle still remains the ethnocentric approach of those who have not yet realised the significance of the CISG and its potential to be a uniform international sales law transcending all legal systems.

Simply put, this book has tried to demonstrate that the availability of tested international jurisprudence supported by academic writing should and has facilitated the development of a unified law. Given the diversity of points of view and exchanges, 'a constant questioning of the existing order at a given moment [has been] conducive to progress [in the achievement of uniformity]'.[420]

419 Charters (2005: 42).
420 Marquis (2005: 56).

Bibliography

Baasch-Anderson, C, 'Furthering the Uniform Application of the CISG, Sources of Law on the Internet' (1998) 10 Pace International Law Review 403–410.

Bailey, J, 'Facing the Truth: Seeing the Convention on Contracts for the International Sale of Goods as an Obstacle to a Uniform Law of International Sales' (1999) 32 Corn ILJ 273.

Basedow, J (ed), *Europäische Vertragsrechtsvereinheitlichung und deutsches Recht*, 2000, Tübingen: Mohr Siebeck.

Bell, G, F, 'Why Singapore Should Withdraw Its [Article 95] Reservation to the United Nations Convention on Contracts for the International Sale of Goods (CISG)' (2005) 9 Singapore Year Book of International Law 55.

Berger, K, P, 'The Principles of European Contract Law and the Concept of the "Creeping Codification" of Law' (2001) 1 European Review of Private Law 21.

Berger, K, P, *The Creeping Codification of the Lex Mercatoria*, 1999, The Hague: Kluwer Law International.

Berger, K, P, Dubberstein, H, Lehmann, S and Petzold, V, 'Anwendung Transnationalen Rechts in der internationalen Vertrags- und Schiedspraxis' (2002) 101 Zeitschrift für vergleichende Zivilrechtswissenschaft 12.

Bianca, C, M and Bonell, M, J, *Commentary on the International Sales Law: The 1980 Vienna Sales Convention*, 1987, Milan: Giuffrè.

Boodman, M, 'The Myth of Harmonisation of Laws' (1991) 39 AJCL 699.

Borisova, B, 'Geographic Sphere of Application of the United Nations Convention on Contracts for the International Sale of Goods' accessed on 18 December 2005, http://xwww.cisg.law.pace.edu/cisg/biblio/borisova.html

Bridge, M, 'Uniformity and Diversity in the Law of International Sales' (2003) 15 Pace International Law Review 55–89.

Bridge, M, '"The Bifocal World of International Sales" Vienna and Non-Vienna', in Cranston, R (ed), *Making Commercial Law: Essays in Honour of Roy Goode*, 1997, Oxford: Clarendon Press, pp 277–297.

Charters, A, 'Fitting the "Situation"; The CISG and the Regulated Market' (2005) 4 Washington University Global Studies Law Review 1.

Conetti, G, 'Uniform Substantive and Conflicts Rules on the International Sale of Goods and Their Interaction', in Šarčević, P and Volken, P (eds), *International Sale of Goods, Dubrovnik Lectures*, 1986, New York: Oceana, pp 385–399.

Cook, S, V, 'CISG from the Perspective of the Practitioner' (1998) 17 Journal of Law and Commerce 343.

De Ly, F, 'Opting Out: Some Observations on the Occasion of the CISG's 25th anniversary', in Ferrari, F (ed), *Quo vadis CISG?*, 2005a, Brussels: Bruylant, pp 25–42.

De Ly, F, 'Sources of International Sales Law: An Eclectic Model', presented in 'Celebrating Success: 25 Years United Nations Convention on Contracts for the International Sale of Goods' at UNCITRAL–SIAC Conference, Singapore, 22–23 September 2005b, accessed on 31 May 2006, http://cisgw3.law.pace.edu/cisg/biblio/dely/html

Dicey, A,V, Morris, J, H, C and Collins, L, *Dicey and Morris on the Conflict of Laws*, 13th edn, 2000, London: Sweet & Maxwell.

Diedrich, F, 'Maintaining Uniformity in International Uniform Law Via Autonomous Interpretation: Software *Contracts* and the CISG' (1996) 8 Pace International Law Review 303.

Diedrich, F, 'Lückenfüllung im Internationalen Einheitsrecht, Möglichkeiten und Grenzen Richterlicher Rechtsfortbildung im Wiener Kaufrecht' (1995) 41 Recht der Internationalen Wirtschaft 353–365.

DiMatteo, L, A, Dhooge, L, Greene, S, Maurer, V and Pagnattaro, M, 'The Interpretative Turn in International Sales Law: An Analysis of Fifteen Years of CISG Jurisprudence' (2004) 34 Northwestern Journal of International Law and Business 299.

Drobnig, U, 'General Principles of European Contract Law', in Šarčević, P and Volken, P (eds), *International Sale of Goods, Dubrovnik Lectures*, 1986, New York: Oceana, 305–332.

Enderlein, F and Maskow, D, *International Sales Law, United Nations Convention on Contracts for the International Sale of Goods*, 1992, New York: Oceana Publications.

Faber, W, 'Zur Richtlinie bezüglich Verbrauchsgüterkauf und Garantien für Verbrauchsgüter' (1999) Juristische Blätter 413.

Farnsworth, A, E, 'Damages and Specific Relief' (1979) 27 AJCL 657.

Felemegas, J, 'The United Nations Convention on Contracts for the International Sale of Goods: Article 7 and Uniform Interpretation' (2003) accessed on 15 November 2005, http://www.cisg.law.pace.edu/cisg/biblio/felemegas.html

Ferrari, F, 'Do Courts Interpret the CISG Uniformly?', in Ferrari, F (ed), *Quo Vadis CISG?*, 2005, Brussels: Bruylant, pp 3–23.

Ferrari, F, ' "Forum Shopping" Despite International Uniform Contract Law Conventions' (2002a) 51 ICLQ 689.

Ferrari, F, 'Zum vertraglichen Ausschluss des UN-Kaufrechts' (2002b) 4 Zeitschrift für Europäisches Privatrecht 737–746.

Ferrari, F, 'Specific Topics of the CISG in the Light of Judicial Application and Scholarly Writing' (1995) 15 Journal of Law and Commerce 1–126.

Flechtner, H, M, 'The Several Texts of the CISG in a Decentralized System: Observations on Translations, Reservations and Other Challenges to the Uniformity Principle in Article 7(1)' (1998) 17 Journal of Law and Commerce 187.

Flechtner, H, M, 'More U.S. Decisions on the U.N. Sales Convention: Scope, Parol Evidence, "Validity" and Reduction of Price under article 50' (1995) 14 Journal of Law and Commerce 153.

Gabriel, H, *Contracts for the Sale of Goods, A Comparison of Domestic and International Law*, 2004, Dobbs Ferry: Oceana.

Glenn, P, 'Unification of Law, Harmonisation of Law and Private International Law', in Erauw, J, Bouckaert, B, Bocken, H, Gaus, H and Storme, M (eds), *Liber Memorialis Francois Laurent 1810–1887*, 1989, Brussels: E. Story-Scientia, pp 783–784.

Hansard, H, L, 3 May 1995, Vol. 563 cols 1457 ff.

Happ, R, 'Anwendbarkeit Völkerrechtlicher Auslegungsmethoden auf das UN-Kaufrecht' (1997) 43 Recht der Internationalen Wirtschaft 376–380.

Hartnell, H, E, 'Rousing the Sleeping Dog: The Validity Exception to the Convention of Contracts for the International Sale of Goods' (1993) 18 Yale Journal of International Law 1.

Herbel, P, 'Der internationale Unternehmensjurist – ein Vaterlandsloser Geselle?', in Schwenzer, I (ed), *Schuldrecht, Rechtsvergleichung und Rechtsvereinheitlichung an der Schwelle zum 21. Jahrhundert: Symposium aus Anlass des 65. Geburtstages von Peter Schlechtriem*, 1999, Tübingen: Mohr Siebeck, pp 1–19.

Herman, S, 'Specific Performance; a Comparative Analysis' (2003) 7 Edinburgh Law Review 5, 194.

Hillman, R, A, 'Cross Reference and Editorial Analysis, Article 7', last update September 1997, 2, http://cisgw3.law.pace.edu/cisg/text/hillman.html

Hillman, R, A, 'Applying the United Nations Convention on Contracts for the International Sale of Goods: The Elusive Goal for Uniformity' (1995) Cornell Review of the Convention on Contracts for the International Sale of Goods, 21 accessed on 10 January 2006, http://cisg3.law.pace.edu/cisg/biblio/hillman/html

Hobhouse, J, S, 'International Conventions and Commercial Law: The Pursuit of Uniformity' (1990) 106 LQR 530.

Honnold, J, *Uniform Law for International Sales Under the 1980 United Nations Convention*, 3rd edn, 1999, The Hague [etc.]: Kluwer Law International.

Honnold, J, 'Uniform Laws for International Trade: Early "Care and Feeding" for Uniform Growth' (1995) 1 International Trade and Business Law Journal 1.

Honnold, J, 'The Sales Convention in Action – Uniform International Words: Uniform Application?' (1988) 8 Journal of Law and Commerce 207–212.

Huber, U, 'Der UNCITRAL-Entwurf eines Übereinkommens über Internationale Warenkaufverträge' (1979) 43 Rabels Zeitschrift 413.

Kastely, A, 'Unification and Community: A Rhetorical Analysis of the United Nations Sales Convention' (1988) 8 Northwestern Journal of International Law and Business 574.

Keily, T, 'Good Faith and the Vienna Convention on Contracts for the International Sale of Goods (CISG)' (1999) 3 Vindobona Journal of International Commercial Law and Arbitration 15.

Kennedy, D, 'Form and Substance' (1976) 89 (8) Harv L Rev 1722.

Khoury, D, 'The Statute of Frauds revisited', September 1990, 64(9) *Law Institute Journal* 822, http://www.businessandlaw.vu.edu.au/cisg/

Kieninger, E-M, *Wettbewerb der Privatrechtsordnungen im Europäischen Binnenmarkt*, 2002, Tübingen: Mohr Siebeck.

Kötz, H, 'Rechtsvereinheitlichung – Nutzen, Kosten, Methoden, Ziele' (1986) 50 Rabels Zeitschrift 1.

Kramer, E, 'Konvergenz und Internationalisierung der juristischen Methode', in Meier-Schatz, C (ed), *Die Zukunft des Rechts*, 1999, Basel: Helbing & Lichtenhahn, pp 71–86.

Kramer, E, 'Uniforme Interpretation von Einheitsprivatrecht – mit besonderer Berücksichtigung von Art 7 UNKR' (1996) Österreichisches Juristische Blätter 137–151.

Kruisinga, S, A, *(Non)conformity in the 1980 UN Convention on the Contracts for the International Sale of Goods: A Uniform Concept?*, 2004, Antwerp: Intersentia.

Lando, O, 'Principles of European Contract Law and UNIDROIT Principles: Moving from Harmonisation to Unification?' (2003) 1/2, Uniform Law Review 125.

Leible, S, 'Aussenhandel und Rechtssicherheit' (1998) 97 Zeitschrift für vergleichende Rechtswissenschaft 286.

Lessiak, R, 'UNCITRAL Kaufrechtsabkommen und Irrtumsanfechtung' (1989) Österreichische Juristische Blätter 487–496.

Leyens, P, 'CISG and Mistake: Uniform Law vs. Domestic Law. The Interpretative Challenge of Mistake and the Validity Loophole' (2003) accessed on 10 August 2005, http://www.cisg.law.pace.edu/cisg/biblio/leyens.html

Linarelli, J, 'Why (Not) Seek Uniform Solutions?' in 'The Economics of Private Law Harmonisation', in Linarelli, J (ed), *Proceedings of the 96th Annual Meeting of the American Society of International Law*, 13–16 March 2002, HeinOnline, pp 339–342.

Lookofsky, J and Flechtner, H, 'Nominating Manfred Forberich: The Worst CISG Decision in 25 Years?' (2005) 9 The Vindobona Journal of International Commercial Law and Arbitration 199.

Lord Bingham 'A New Common Law for Europe', in Markesinis, B (ed), *The Clifford Chance Millenium Lectures, the Coming Together of the Common Law and the Civil Law*, 2000, Oxford: Hart Publishing.

Magnus, U, *Wiener UN-Kaufrecht (CISG), J. von Staudingers Kommentar zum Bürgerlichen Gesetzbuch mit Einführungsgesetz und Nebengesetzen*, 2005, Berlin: Sellier – de Gruyter.

Magnus, U, in Schwenzer, I (ed), *Schuldrecht, Rechtsvergleichung und Rechtsvereinheitlichung an der Schwelle zum 21. Jahrhundert: Symposium aus Anlass des 65. Geburtstages von Peter Schlechtriem*, 1999, Tübingen: Mohr Siebeck 25.

Magnus, U, 'Währungsfragen im Einheitlichen Kaufrecht. Zugleich ein Beitrag zu seiner Lückenfüllung und Auslegung' (1989) 53 Rabels Zeitschrift 116.

Marquis, L, *International Uniform Commercial Law, Towards a Progressive Consciousness*, 2005, Aldershot: Ashgate.

Martiny, D, 'Traditional Private and Commercial Law Rules under the Pressure of Global Transactions: The Role for an International Order', in Appelbaum, R, Felstiner, W and Gessner, V (eds), *Rules and Networks: The Legal Culture of Global Business Transactions*, 2001, Oxford: Hart Publishing, pp 123–155.

Mather, H, 'Choice of law for International Sales Issues Not Resolved by the CISG' (2001) 20 Journal of Law and Commerce 155.

Merryman, J, 'On the Convergence (and Divergence) of the Civil Law and the Common Law', in Cappelletti, M (ed), *New Perspectives for a Common Law of Europe*, 1978, Leiden, London, Boston: Sijthoff [etc.], Publications of the European University Institute, pp 195–236.

Murray, J, Jr, 'The Revision of Article 2: Romancing the Prism' (1994) 35 William and Mary Law Review 1447.

Nhlapo, R, 'Keynote by the Chairman of the Joint ALI/UNIDROIT Study Group' (2004) 4 Uniform Law Review 811.

Nicholas, B, 'The United Kingdom and the Vienna Sales Convention: Another case of Splendid Isolation?', presented at Saggi, conferenze e Seminari, centro di studi e recherché di diritto comparato e straniero, Series No 9, 3 (1993) accessed on 24 November 2005, http://soi.cnr.it/~crdcs/crdcs/nicholas.htm

Pauly, C, 'The Concept of Fundamental Breach as An International Principle to Create Uniformity of Commercial Law' (2000) 19 Journal of Law and Commerce 221.

Pfeiffer, T, 'Systemdenken im neuen Leistungsstörungs- und Gewährleistungsrecht' (2002) Zeitschrift für das gesamte Schuldrecht 23.

Pribetic, A, ' "Bringing Locus in Focus": A Choice-of-Law Methodology for CISG-based Concurrent Contract and Product Liability Claims', 2004 accessed on 9 February 2006, http://www.cisg.law.pace.edu/cisg/biblio/pribetic1.html

Rabel, E, 'The Hague Conference on the Unification of Sales Law' (1952) 1 AJCL 58.

Rabel, E, 'Der Entwurf eines einheitlichen Kaufgesetzes' (1935) 9 Rabels Zeitschrift 1.

Raff, M, J, 'German real property law and the conclusive land title register', unpublished PhD thesis, 1999 University of Melbourne.

Rolland, W, 'Schuldrechtsreform – Allgemeiner Teil' (1992) Neue Juristische Wochenschrift 2377.

Rosett, A, 'The UNIDROIT Principles of International Commercial Contracts: A New Approach to International Commercial Contracts' (1998) 46 AJCL Supplement 347.

Rosett, A, 'The International Sales Convention: A Dissenting View' (1984) 18 International Lawyer 445.

Sautet, M, *Un Café pour Socrate*, 1995, Paris: Robert Laffont.

Schlechtriem, P, *Internationales UN-Kaufrecht*, 3rd edn, 2005, Tübingen: Mohr Siebeck.

Schlechtriem, P, 'The German Act to Modernize the Law of Obligations in the Context of Common Principles and Structures of the Law of Obligations in Europe' (2002) Oxford University Comparative Law Forum 2, http://ouclf.iuscomp.org/articles/schlechtriem2.shtml

Schlechtriem, P, 'Uniform Sales Law – The Experience with Uniform Sales Laws in the Federal Republic of Germany' (1991) Juridisk Tidskrift vid Stockholm Universitet 1.

Schlechtriem, P, 'The Borderland of Tort and Contract – Opening a new Frontier?' (1988) 21 Cornell International Law Journal 467.

Schlechtriem, P and Schwenzer, I (eds), *Commentary on the UN Convention on the International Sale of Goods (CISG)*, 2nd edn, 2005, Oxford: Oxford University Press.

Schlechtriem, P and Schwenzer, I (eds), *Kommentar zum Einheitlichen UN-Kaufrecht (CISG)*, 4th edn, 2004, München: Verlag C.H. Beck.

Schwartz, A and Scott, R, 'The Political Economy of Private Legislatures' (1994) 143 University of Pennsylvania Law Review 595.

Schwenzer, I, 'The Danger of Domestic Pre-Conceived Views with Respect to the Uniform Interpretation of the CISG: The Question of Avoidance in the Case of Non-Conforming Goods and Documents' (2005) 36 (4) Victoria University of Wellington Law Review 795.

Schwenzer, I, *Schweizerisches Obligationenrecht Allgemeiner Teil*, 2nd edn, 2000, Bern: Stämpfli Verlag.

Sinclair, I, *The Vienna Convention on the Law of Treaties*, 2nd edn, 1984, Manchester: University Press.

Smits, J, 'Diversity of Contract Law and the European Internal Market', in Smits, J (ed), *The Need for a European Contract Law, Empirical and Legal Perspectives*, 2005, Groningen: Europa Law Publishing 155–179.

Speidel, R, 'The Revision of the UCC Article 2, Sales in the Light of the United Nations Convention on Contracts for the International Sale of Goods' (1995) 16 Northwestern Journal of International Laws and Business 165.

Speidel, R, 'Buyer's Remedies of Rejection and Cancellation under the UCC and the Convention' (1993) 6 The Journal of Contract Law 131–140.

Stadie, V and Nietzer, W, 'CISG – Das UN-Kaufrecht in der Anwaltspraxis' (2002) 43 Monatsschrift für Deutsches Recht 428–433.

Staudenmayer, D, 'Die EG-Richtlinie über den Verbrauchsgüterkauf' (1999) Neue Juristische Wochenschrift 2393.

Stein, E, 'Uses, Misuses – and Nonuses of Comparative Law' (1977) 72 Northwestern UL Rev, 198.

Stephan, P, 'The Futility of Unification and Harmonization in International Commercial Law' (1999) 39 Virginia Journal of International Law 743.

Thiele, C, 'Interest on Damages and Rate of Interest Under Article 78 of the U.N. Convention on Contracts for the International Sale of Goods' (1998) 2 Vindobona Journal of International Commercial Law and Arbitration 3.

Volken, P, 'The Vienna Convention: Scope, Interpretation, Gap-filling', in Šarčević, P and Volken, P (eds), *International Sale of Goods, Dubrovnik Lectures*, 1986, New York: Oceana, pp 19–53.

Walker, J, 'The Better Part of Harmonizing Jurisdictional Law', in Linarelli, J (ed), *Proceedings of the 96th Annual Meeting of the American Society of International Law,* 13–16 March 2002, HeinOnline, pp 342–347.

Walt, S, 'Novelty and the Risk of Uniform Sales Law' (1999) 39 Virginia Journal of International Law 671.

Watson, A, 'Comparative Law and Legal Change' [1978] CLJ 313.

Watson, A, *Legal Transplants: An Approach to Comparative Law*, 1974, Edinburgh: Scottish Academic Press.

Whincop, M and Keyes, M, 'Putting the "Private" Back into Private International Law: Default Rules and the Proper Law of the Contract' (1997) Melbourne UL Rev, 515.

Wilhelm, J, 'Die Pflichtverletzung nach dem neuen Schuldrecht' (2004) Juristenzeitung 1055.

Zeller, B, *Damages under the Convention on Contracts for the International Sale of Goods*, 2005, Dobbs Ferry: Oceana Press.

Zeller, B, 'Four-Corners – The Methodology for Interpretation and Application of the UN Convention on Contracts for the International Sale of Goods', 2003, accessed on 20 July 20, 2005, http://www.cisg.law.pace.edu/cisg/biblio/4corners.html

Zeller, B, 'Jurisdiction in Cyberspace; Does the CISG "Manage the GCM"?' (2002) 6 Vindobona Journal of International Commercial Law and Arbitration 305.

Ziegel, J, 'Report to the Uniform Law Conference of Canada on Convention on Contracts for the International Sale of Goods' (1981) accessed on 25 July 2005, http://www.cisg.law.pace.edu/cisg/text/ziegel4.html

Zweigert, K and Kötz, H, *Introduction to Comparative Law*, 3rd edn, 1998, Oxford: Clarendon Press.

Index

For Product Safety Concerns and Information please contact our EU representative GPSR@taylorandfrancis.com
Taylor & Francis Verlag GmbH, Kaufingerstraße 24, 80331 München, Germany

www.ingramcontent.com/pod-product-compliance
Ingram Content Group UK Ltd.
Pitfield, Milton Keynes, MK11 3LW, UK
UKHW011020180926
475701UK00004B/845
9780415421737